MW00812340

Private Equity Funds in China

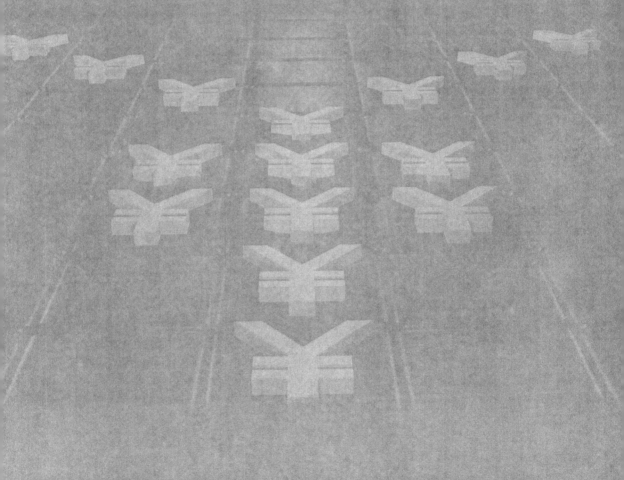

Private Equity Funds in China:
A 20-Year Overview
Volume 2

Edited by Xia Bin,
Wang Changyun, and Zhou Ye'an

Enrich Professional Publishing

Singapore • Hong Kong • Beijing • Honolulu

Published by

Enrich Professional Publishing (S) Private Limited
16L, Enterprise Road,
Singapore 627660
Website: www.enrichprofessional.com
A Member of Enrich Culture Group Limited

Hong Kong Head Office:

2/F, Rays Industrial Building, 71 Hung To Road, Kwun Tong, Kowloon, Hong Kong, China

China Office:

Rm 309, Building A, Central Valley, 16 Hai Dian Zhong Jie, Haidian District, Beijing, China

United States Office:

PO Box 30812, Honolulu, HI 96820, USA

English edition © 2014 by Enrich Professional Publishing (S) Private Limited
Chinese original edition © 2011 by China Renmin University Press

Translated by Vivien Lee

Edited by Glenn Griffith and Vivien Lee

All rights reserved. This book, or parts thereof, may not be reproduced in any form or by any means, electronic or mechanical, including photocopying, recording or any information storage and retrieval system now known or to be invented, without prior written permission from the Publisher.

ISBN   978-1-62320-007-7

This publication is designed to provide accurate and authoritative information in regard to the subject matter covered. It is sold with the understanding that the publisher is not engaged in rendering legal, accounting, or other professional service. If legal advice or other expert assistance is required, the services of a competent professional person should be sought.

Enrich Professional Publishing is an independent globally-minded publisher focusing on the econmic and financial developments that have revolutionized New China. We aim to serve the needs of advanced degree students, researchers, and business professionals who are looking for authoritative, accurate, and engaging information on China.

Printed in Hong Kong with woodfree paper from Japan

Editorial Board (Chinese Edition)

Chief Editor

Xia Bin
Counselor, State Council
Member, Monetary Policy Committee, People's Bank of China
Honorary Director General, Financial Research Institute, Development Research
Center of the State Council

Deputy Chief Editors

Wang Changyun
Professor, School of Finance, Renmin University of China
Director, China Financial Policy Research Center, Renmin University of China

Zhou Ye'an
Professor, School of Economics, Renmin University of China

Executive Chief Editors

Yang Hui
Chairman of the board, HMCF Investment Holding Co., Ltd.

Yang Qijing
Professor, School of Economics, Renmin University of China
Executive Director, Center of Firm and Organization Studies, Renmin University
of China

Editorial Committee Members

Chen Daofu
Deputy Director, Comprehensive Research Office, Financial Research Institute,
Development Research Center of the State Council

Guo Jie
Professor and Vice Dean, School of Economics, Renmin University of China

He Gang
Executive Chief Editor, *Caijing Magazine*

Li Tao
Professor and Vice Dean, School of Economics, Central University of Finance and Economics

Liao Li
Professor and Vice Dean, School of Economics and Management, Tsinghua University

Lu Jianping
Professor and Executive Vice Dean, College for Criminal Law Science, Beijing Normal University

Sun Jianfang
Chief Reporter and Member of the Editorial Board, *Economic Observer*

Tang Hongxin
Partner of Yingke Law Firm

Wang Yan
President (China Region), Bridgewater Associates, LP

Wu Weixing
Professor and Vice Dean, School of Banking and Finance, University of International Business and Economics

Zhu Wuxiang
Deputy Director, Department of Finance, School of Economics and Management, Tsinghua University

Editors and Contributors

From HMCF Investment Holding Co., Ltd.:

Li Xinyue	Xie Fei	Zhang Yixuan
Pan Xiaomin	Yan Xiaojia	

From the Renmin University of China:

Liu Wei	Wang Mengyu
Liu Wei	Zhan Mengqi

Contents

Chapter 5 Analysis of the Environment for the Regulation
of Private Funds 1

Chapter 6 Analysis of the Development of China's
Privately Offered Fund Industry 37

Chapter 7 Analysis of the Current Situation of China's
Private Securities Investment Fund Companies 95

Chapter 8 Analysis of Private
Non-Securities Investment Funds 135

Chapter 9 Recommendations on the Development of
China's Privately Offered Funds 159

Notes 167

Bibliography 169

Index 177

5

Chapter

Analysis of the Environment for the Regulation of Private Funds

China's privately offered funds began to develop rather late compared to other markets, but their development has been rapid and the privately offered funds industry is starting to take shape, thanks to the soaring economy and growth of the capital market. However, the current regulatory system is chaotic and unstandardized. With China's financial markets gradually opening up and the emergence of financial derivatives, hedge funds are expected to grow more rapidly; a poor regulatory system would become more detrimental to the stability of the financial markets. Therefore, a well-developed, effective, and standardized regulatory system must be imposed on the privately offered funds to facilitate the progression of the industry.

Regulatory Systems of Private Funds in Mature Markets

The U.S. regulatory system of investment funds

The U.S. is the country with the most well-developed and oldest fund industry in the world. In 2010, 48% of global mutual funds and 68% of global hedge funds were based in the U.S. The first U.S. investment company was founded in 1825. Before 1926, investment companies were insignificant in the U.S. financial industry. Funds were in their infancy. In 1911, Kansas announced the first regulatory law on securities (blue sky law). Many states followed suit. However, individual legislation could not effectively combat fraud. Since 1926, the development of investment companies accelerated. In three years, more than 600 were set up. Before the Wall Street Crash of 1929, the total assets of the investment companies reached USD8 billion. At that time, investment companies were unregulated. Some of them took advantage of small investors. The Wall Street Crash of 1929 crushed the reputation of investment companies. The exploration of the legal regulation of investment companies began.

The legislation process of the U.S. funds began with the financial reform after the Great Depression (1929–1939). The *Securities Act of 1933*, the *Securities Exchange Act of 1934*, the *Investment Company Act of 1940*, and the *Investment Advisers Act of 1940* were issued. The fund industry became subject to financial regulation, although private funds were exempt from the law. Since the first hedge fund emerged in 1950, U.S. private funds have been constantly investing in high-leverage derivatives. In the Sterling crisis, the Mexican peso crisis, the Asian financial crisis, and the 2008 global economic crisis, hedge funds played a role in aggravating and accelerating the crises while employing high leverage.

After suffering the 2008 global crisis, the U.S. began financial regulation reform. In 2010, the *Dodd-Frank Wall Street Reform and Consumer Protection Act* was announced. It stipulated that the regulation of private funds should be strengthened.

Regulatory system of mutual funds

U.S. mutual funds are under legal restrictions and are regulated by the Securities and Exchange Commission (SEC). The SEC possesses quasi-judicial powers and quasi-legislative powers. It oversees the offerings and trading activities of funds as well as the operating activities of fund institutions in order to protect investors.

Under such a system, self-regulation is important in the industry. The Financial Industry Regulatory Authority (FINRA), the Investment Company Institute (ICI), and various securities exchanges are examples of self-regulatory bodies of the industry. FINRA was established in July 2007 through the consolidation of the National Association of Securities Dealers (NASD) and the member regulation, enforcement, and arbitration operations of the New York Stock Exchange. FINRA is an independent, non-government regulator of securities companies. It safeguards fairness in the U.S. capital market and protects investors through regulating securities companies, educating investors, and alerting investors to investment risks.

The U.S. fund industry has a long history and its legal regulatory system is more complete. The system can be separated into two tiers. The first tier is the Federal legal system, which issued laws including the *Securities Act of 1933*, the *Securities Exchange Act of 1934*, the *Investment Company Act of 1940*, and the *Investment Advisers Act of 1940*. The second tier is the state-level system. Most of the states have announced securities laws.

Regulatory system of private funds

In the U.S., private funds and mutual funds are under the same investment fund regulatory system. Before the 2008 global financial crisis, private funds were self-regulated with legal exemption. The announcement of the *Dodd-Frank Wall Street Reform and Consumer Protection Act* in 2010 brought significant changes to the financial regulatory system. Through legislation and establishing a two-tier regulatory system, the government monitors the private fund markets.

At present, the regulators of hedge funds include the SEC, the Financial Stability Oversight Council (FSOC), and the state governments which are responsible for the registration and information disclosure of private funds. The FSOC was established after the global financial crisis and during financial reform and it mainly regulates non-bank financial institutions. The FSOC collects data and analyzes potential risks. It recommended that the Federal Reserve tighten the regulations on capital, leverage, fluidity, and risk management. It reports to the U.S. Congress and releases its reports to the public every year.

There was not any specific law on private funds in the U.S., and private funds were exempt from the *Securities Act of 1933*, the *Investment Company Act of 1940*, and the *Investment Advisers Act of 1940*. Section 4 of the *Securities Act of 1933* stipulates that "transactions by an issuer not involving any public offering" are exempted from the law. Section 3 of the *Investment Company Act of 1940* stipulates that non-public offering investment vehicles which are beneficially owned by not more than 100 persons or offered to purchasers are exempt from the law. Section 203 of the *Investment Advisers Act of 1940* stipulates that private fund managers in the U.S. shall be exempt from registration.[1]

As private funds continued to grow, in 1982, the SEC refined Regulation D in the *Securities Act of 1933* to be more precise. Rule 506 under Regulation D was considered a "safe harbor" for private funds. According to the rule, a company can raise an unlimited amount of capital as long as the following standards are fulfilled:

- The company cannot use general solicitation or advertising to market the securities.
- The company may sell its securities to an unlimited number of "accredited investors" and up to 35 other purchases…. All non-accredited investors … must have … sufficient knowledge and experience in financial and business matters to make them capable of evaluating the merits and risks of the prospective investment.
- Companies must decide what information to give to accredited investors, so long as it does not violate the antifraud prohibitions of the federal securities laws. But companies must give non-accredited investors disclosure documents that are generally the same as those used in registered offerings. If a company provides information to accredited investors, it must make this information available to non-accredited investors as well.

While companies which satisfy these standards need not register with the SEC, they are required to submit Form D to the SEC after they sell their securities for the first time. Before 2009, the U.S. private fund regulatory system was mainly based on conditional exemption under a well-developed securities regulatory system. The regulation of private funds was relatively lenient and it depended on self-regulation of the industry.[2]

In July 21, 2010, the *Dodd-Frank Wall Street Reform and Consumer Protection Act* passed by Congress and signed by President Obama came into effect. Title IV defined "private funds" and revised the regulations on private funds. The main points are as follows:

- Private adviser exemption is eliminated.
- Private advisers are required to maintain such records of, and file with the Commission such reports regarding, private funds advised by the investment adviser or for the assessment of systemic risk by the Financial Stability Oversight Council.
- Exemption of venture capital fund advisers: No investment adviser that acts as an investment adviser solely to one or more venture capital funds shall be subject to the registration requirements of this title with respect to the provision of investment advice relating to a venture capital fund.
- The Commission shall provide an exemption from the registration requirements under this section to any investment adviser of private funds, if each of such investment advisers acts solely as an adviser to private funds and has assets under management in the United States of less than USD150 million.
- Family offices are exempt from registration and information disclosure.
- An investment adviser registered shall safeguard and verify client assets by an independent public accountant abiding by the rules of the SEC.
- Shift in federal and state responsibilities: Private fund investment advisers with assets under management over USD100 million shall be regulated by the SEC; those with assets under management under USD100 million shall be regulated by the state.[3]

In June 2011, the SEC passed the proposal to include hedge funds under regulation. According to the new regulations, hedge funds and private equity management companies which have assets under management over USD150 million, or more than 15 clients, shall register with the SEC.

The regulatory system has become more stringent after reform. Hedge fund managers took actions to maintain their status of exemption. Business magnate George Soros announced on July 27, 2011, the closure of his funds to outside investors and that he would convert his hedge fund company to a home business so as to enjoy exemption.

The U.K. regulatory system of investment funds

The U.K. is the birthplace of the fund industry. As the financial center of Europe, London sees 69% of European hedge fund transactions take place there. It is also the largest European fund market. The U.K. regulatory system of investment funds has a long history.

The U.K. gained wealth through the Industrial Revolution and the profits from the colonies of the U.K. The gains brought about by domestic capital investment were dropping. Capital was flowing to overseas markets. This was when investment funds began to emerge. Due to the lack of legal protection, frauds within funds were common. In order to regulate the fund industry, the government intervened and announced the *Companies Act 1879* to amend the law with respect to joint stock companies. The development of funds began to be regulated by law. After the Great Depression in 1929, like other countries, the U.K. tightened its regulation of the financial industry. In the late 1970s, Margaret Thatcher took office and advocated the policies of an open economy. The *Financial Service Act 1986* marked the beginning of the practice of financial liberalization. The U.K. fund industry entered into a period of rapid growth in the 1980s. The lack of stringent regulatory measures during financial liberalization presented opportunities for financial speculation. This forced the U.K. government to reform its financial regulatory system in 1997 and established the Financial Service Agency. The *Financial Service Act 1986* was revoked and the *Financial Services and Markets Act 2000* was announced. Under the new *Act*, private funds were exempt. After the 2008 global financial crisis, many countries included private funds in the regulatory system. The U.K. announced new laws in 2010 and private funds are now required to disclose information.

European Integration after the Second World War influenced the fund industry regulation in the U.K. The U.K. joined the European Union (EU) in 1973. This meant that the U.K. needs to abide by the laws of the EU in both political and economic aspects.

In the U.K., investment funds are called collective investment schemes, and they are categorized into regulated and unregulated ones, which are counterparts to public funds and private funds, respectively.

Regulated collective investment schemes

The regulation of regulated collective investment schemes is centralized to the government. The structure of the regulatory system can be divided into three broad levels[4]:

(1) The EU introduced the *Undertakings for Collective Investment in Transferable Securities Directive* (UCITS Directive). A collective investment scheme authorized by any of the member states which complies with the UCITS Directive's provisions can be promoted throughout the European Economic Area.

(2) The U.K. government is mainly responsible for formulating the political and legal framework for the regulation of the collective investment schemes. The main government legislation includes: the *Financial Services and Markets Act 2000* and its relevant second-tier regulations, and the *Open-Ended Investment Companies Regulations* (OEIC Regulations).

(3) The Financial Services Authority (FSA) is the executive institution for the regulation of collective investment schemes with powers conferred by the government. The FSA is a non-government limited liability company. Its channel of capital includes the companies under its regulation. Its board of directors was appointed by the HM Treasury. It reports directly to the HM Treasury.

Other than the EU, the U.K. government, and the FSA, there are independent regulatory bodies, including the Investment Management Association and the London Stock Exchange.

Unregulated collective investment schemes

Before the 2008 global financial crisis, unregulated collective investment schemes relied on self-regulation of the industry. After the crisis, the government gradually included unregulated collective investment schemes into its regulation.

There is not an explicit definition of private funds in the U.K. According to Section 238 of the *Financial Services and Markets Act 2000*, regulated collective investment schemes are authorized by the government and allowed to be promoted to the public. They mainly include funds authorized by the government and established in the U.K., and collective investment schemes established overseas and authorized by the FSA. Investment schemes which do not satisfy at least one of the requirements are considered unregulated investment schemes.

The *Financial Services and Markets Act 2000* exempted the collective investment schemes — which are not offered to the public — from registration, and they are not under the FSA's regulation. The *Promotion of Collective Investment Schemes (Exemptions) Order* of the *Financial Services and*

Markets Act 2000 offers more precise definitions of collective investment schemes which can enjoy exemption from the aspects of communications and investors. "Communication" refers to "the communication, by an authorized person in the course of business, of an invitation or inducement to participate in an unregulated scheme." Communication is categorized into "real-time communication" and "non-real-time communication." Real-time communication is further categorized into "solicited real-time communication" and "unsolicited real-time communication."

In non-real-time communication or solicited real-time communication, the following parties can enjoy exemption: overseas individuals; investment professionals; existing participants in an unregulated scheme; certified high-net-worth individuals (HNWIs); high-net-worth companies and unincorporated associations; sophisticated investors; associations of high-net-worth or sophisticated investors; settlors, trustees, and personal representatives; beneficiaries of trust, will, or intestacy; and persons placing promotional material in particular publications. The following forms of communication are also exempt: communication with only one investor or investment company; and communication of other investment schemes authorized by other legislation.

Unsolicited real-time communication can only be conducted for the following parties: overseas individuals; investment professionals; high-net-worth companies and unincorporated associations; sophisticated investors; settlors, trustees, and personal representatives; beneficiaries of trust, will, or intestacy; and persons placing promotional material in particular publications. Communication of other investment schemes authorized by other legislation is exempt.[5]

After the shock from the 2008 global financial crisis, the U.K. government passed the new *Financial Services Act* on April 8, 2010. The new *Financial Services Act* amended the *Financial Services and Markets Act 2000* and bestowed new authority and objectives to the FSA. Section 18 of the *Financial Services Act* provides clear requirements for information disclosure regarding transactions in the U.K. and the investment funds offered by legal persons in the U.K. (e.g., long-only funds, hedge funds, and private equity funds): If the FSA deems certain information important for maintaining the stability of the U.K. financial system, it can request the investment fund managers or investors to provide the corresponding information.[6]

At that time, the U.K. was preparing for the launch of new financial regulators. The FSA was abolished in April 2013 and replaced by the following bodies: the Financial Policy Committee for macroeconomic regulation; the

Prudential Regulation Authority for microeconomic regulation; the Consumer Protection and Markets Authority for consumer protection and market regulation; and the Serious Economic Crime Agency.

The U.K. does not require private collective investment schemes to register. In 2010, the U.K. was against the EU's amendments to the *UCITS Directive*. The proposed revision was that private funds with over EUR500 million and hedge funds with over USD1 million should register with regulators before they could operate in the European Economic Area.

Hong Kong's regulatory system of investment funds

As one of the global financial centers, Hong Kong's capital market is highly international. Hong Kong's stock exchange and foreign exchange rank among the top in the world. Hong Kong is also the largest venture capital (VC) center. Its fund industry is well developed. The influence of its capital market is sizable in Asia and around the world.

Before the Handover in 1997, the regulation of the Hong Kong investment fund industry was administered and bound by the legislation of the U.K. After 1997, hedge funds such as Soros's Quantum Fund entered the Hong Kong market and began an economic war with the Hong Kong government. After the war, Hong Kong began the legislation process concerning financial securities. The *Code on Unit Trusts and Mutual Funds* was revised, and the *Securities and Futures Ordinance* was announced in 2003. After the 2008 global financial crisis through the time of this writing, Hong Kong has not reformed its regulatory system of investment funds.

Regulatory system of public funds

Hong Kong's public funds are regulated by the government as well as by the industry itself. The Securities and Futures Commission (SFC) of Hong Kong is the highest authority over Hong Kong's securities investment funds. It is an independent statutory body which regulates the securities and futures markets in Hong Kong.

Self-regulatory bodies included the Hong Kong Investment Funds Association (HKIFA) and the Hong Kong Stock Exchange. The HKIFA is a non-profit-making association of the Hong Kong fund industry with a view to educate investors and facilitate communications among members. Its missions are as follows[7]:

> • To foster the development of the fund management industry in Hong Kong;

- To enhance the professional standards of the industry to ensure that they are in line with international best practices; and
- To maintain Hong Kong's competitiveness as the major fund management center in Asia.

Hong Kong's legislation on investment fund regulation includes the *Securities and Futures Ordinance* and the *Code on Unit Trusts and Mutual Funds*. The *Securities and Futures Ordinance* came into effect on April 1, 2003. It combined 10 previous regulations on the securities and futures markets. It ensures the regulation of the securities and futures markets and that the market themselves are fair, efficient, and transparent. Investment funds in Hong Kong are called "collective investment schemes" in legal terms (Definitions given in Section 393). Regulations on advertisements, invitations, or documents of collective investments are detailed in Sections 103 and 104. The *Code on Unit Trusts and Mutual Funds* is the legal basis for the regulation of the investment fund industry in Hong Kong.

Regulatory system of private funds

The private funds in Hong Kong are regulated by the SFC and the industry itself. According to Section 213 of the *Securities and Futures Ordinance*, private fund managers who are engaged in the trading of securities and futures should possess relevant licenses in order to perform trading. The legislation of Hong Kong does not require private funds to register or disclose information. The regulations in those aspects are rather slack.

Regulatory system of hedge funds

In May 2002, the SFC published the *Hedge Funds Guidelines*. Later, it issued the *Guidelines on Hedge Funds Reporting Requirements* which regulates the information disclosure of hedge funds. Despite appearing in the appendixes of the *Code on Unit Trusts and Mutual Funds*, the two documents are some of the rare documents which detail the legal requirements of hedge funds. Even in the U.S. where hedge funds are very well developed, there is no legal distinction between hedge funds and mutual funds. Both types of funds are regarded as exempt funds in the *Securities Act*, the *Investment Company Act*, and the *Investment Advisers Act*. There are no laws specific to hedge funds.

The development of the Hong Kong hedge funds is uncommon. Hedge funds can be offered to the public as long as they satisfy some special requirements by the law. These are called public hedge funds. Hedge funds can be classified as either authorized or unauthorized according to the SFC. Authorized hedge funds are restricted by the *Hedge Funds Guidelines* and the *Guidelines on Hedge Funds Reporting Requirements*. They can be publicly offered if the requirements are satisfied. Unauthorized hedge funds cannot be offered to the public and are not restricted by the two documents.

The *Hedge Funds Guidelines* is only applicable to hedge funds which are registered with and authorized by the SFC. It includes clear, detailed requirements regarding the fund manager, the minimum subscription amount, investment and loans, performance fee, call provisions, asset valuation, financial reports, and offering document.

A strict information disclosure system is a feature of the Hong Kong hedge fund regime. As public offerings involve a greater number of investors, information disclosure should be reinforced. The *Guidelines on Hedge Funds Reporting Requirements* details the requirements for information disclosure of public hedge funds. The SFC encourages the disclosure of appropriate information to the hedge fund investors. Authorized hedge funds are required to publish annual reports, semi-annual reports, and quarterly reports. The timeframe for filing and distribution to holders and the contents of the reports are specified.

In fact, there are only five public hedge funds in the Hong Kong market. Most of the hedge funds are private funds, which are not bound by the law. Hong Kong's regulation of hedge funds can act as reference for China's regulation of privately offered funds.

Japan's regulatory system of investment funds

Since its emergence, the investment fund industry of Japan has shouldered the responsibly to revive the economy and provide financial collective asset management. In the 1950s, the Japanese government launched public funds in the form of contract type securities investment trusts in an attempt to revive the economy. Given a stringent regulatory system, in the 40 years of development after the 1950s, private funds (trusts) were not legally recognized.

In the 1990s, Japan implemented financial reform and revised the *Act on Investment Trusts and Investment Corporations*. Private investment trusts were granted legal status and developed rapidly. The regulations on investment trusts are very strict.

Regulatory system of public funds

Japan's regulation of investment trusts are conducted on the basis of the *Act on Investment Trusts and Investment Corporations* and the *Financial Instruments and Exchange Act.* The investment trusts are regulated by the Financial Services Agency. When an investment trust is set up, it must submit a declaration to the local financial agency. The *Financial Instruments and Exchange Act* requires all parties which are engaged in financial exchange to register with the Financial Services Agency and the Ministry of Finance. Unregistered exchange activities are considered a violation of the *Financial Instruments and Exchange Act* and are subject to criminal penalties.

Besides government bodies, the self-regulatory Investment Trusts Association, Japan, also oversees the investment trust industry.

Regulatory system of private funds

Private funds (trusts) in Japan can be categorized into three types.

Privately placed to qualified institutional investors

The *Financial Instruments and Exchange Act* prescribes that qualified institutional investors are investors who have "expert knowledge of and experience with investment in securities." They include parties who are engaged in financial commodity exchange, banks, insurance companies, Shinkin banks and their association, labor banks and their association, the Norinchukin Bank, and the Shoko Chukin Bank.

Privately placed to professional investors

Professional investors include qualified institutional investors, the state, and the Bank of Japan.

Privately placed to general investors

This type of private investment trusts is offered to fewer than 50 investors.

Private investment trusts offered to qualified institutional investors sometimes also include those offered to professional investors. As the investors of such types of trusts are regulated by the Financial Services Agency, these types of trusts are not strictly regulated. On the contrary, the investment trusts offered to general investors are under stricter regulation. Japan's investment trusts are required to detail information about principal, profit allocation, evaluation of trust assets, and leverage in their contracts. All contracts must be submitted to the Prime Minister.

As Japan gradually opened its capital market and allowed for economic liberalization, it began to relax the regulations on the investment trust industry. Japan does not follow the U.S. or Europe in this regard.

Evaluation and comparison of the regulatory environment for private funds in mature markets

The regulatory environment for private funds in the U.S., the U.K., Hong Kong, and Japan differ to various extents. Private funds in these locations influence the development of the fund industry. Below we focus on the system and the regulations in the evaluation and comparison of the regulatory environment.

Comparison of the regulatory system

United States

As a nation of immigrants, the U.S. advocates democracy, liberty, and privacy. It practices market economy. It allows the invisible hand to regulate the market. The market participants shall abide by the legal regulations on the market. Government organizations perform their legal duties to oversee the market in order to prevent market failure.

The characteristics of the U.S. economy are manifested in the regulatory system of investment funds. The regulatory system was established on the basis of a two-tiered legal system. The scope of regulation is well defined, and the market is allowed to self-regulate. After the 2008 global financial crisis, in order to regain control of the market, the U.S. reduced the scope of exemption and imposed tighter regulations on large private funds. It also implemented information disclosure requirements on private funds different than those of the public funds.

The U.S. has the largest private fund industry in the world. The two-tier system raises the efficiency of regulation in monitoring the huge industry.

United Kingdom

As one of the oldest capitalist countries in the world and a member of the EU, the U.K. market economy system is bound by the law of the U.K. and the EU. The legislation of the EU strongly influences the U.K.'s regulation of the fund industry. The U.K. must take into account the law of the EU during its own legislation process.

The U.K.'s regulation of the fund industry is more relaxed than that of the U.S. The laws are less precise and the boundary for exemptions is blurry. After the 2008 global financial crisis, the U.K. was against the EU's amendments to the *UCITS Directive*. The U.K.'s new proposal of regulations on information disclosure was rather general without precise details like the *Dodd-Frank Wall Street Reform and Consumer Protection Act* of the U.S.

As the U.K. private fund market is much smaller than that of the U.S., the FSA was the only private fund regulator in the U.K. [until April 2003]. The allocation of regulatory authority is more concentrated compared to that of the U.S.

Hong Kong

The politics and legislation were influenced by and resemble those of the U.K. As one of the most open economies in the world, Hong Kong relies on its financial industry to be the backbone of its economy. Any fluctuations of the financial industry might cause huge damage to the local economy. As early as 1998, after the Asian Financial Crisis, Hong Kong reformed its regulatory system of investment funds. It imposed strict regulations on both public and private funds. The requirements for the launch and withdrawal of funds are described in such detail that even the U.S. or the U.K. cannot match the legislation. As for hedge funds, the entry restrictions and information disclosure requirements are stringent for public hedge funds. The regulation of private funds remains relative lenient.

The size of Hong Kong's private funds market is much smaller than that in the U.S. and the U.K. The Securities and Futures Commission is the single regulator of private funds in Hong Kong.

Japan

Japan, a country with a statutory law system, has always adopted a bank-oriented financial system. The main bank system was hugely effective in reviving the economy in the post-war period. However, the flaws of the system, such as the soft budget constraint and the government/enterprise relationship being too cozy, put Japan in a period of difficulties after many years of economic growth. At the same time, economic growth drove up the family income rapidly. Many high-net-worth individuals (HNWIs) emerged. Their demand for wealth management needed to be satisfied. In view of this, the Japanese government began to accelerate marketization of the financial market. Through encouraging the development of financial institutions, especially public and investment trusts, the households' diversified demand for wealth management was satisfied, and assets allocation and the institutional structure were optimized.

As the Japanese government regards private trusts as targeting the HNWIs, it imposes relatively slack regulations on them in comparison to those on the public funds. This is to allow private trusts to have a stronger innovative capability and competitive edge while maintaining the order of the industry. Different from the U.S. and the U.K., the Japanese government intervenes in the market. It directs the development of financial institutions. However, compared to the markets of statutory countries such as France and Germany, the control of the Japanese government over the markets is not as rigorous.

Overall, Japan has a more stringent regulation of private funds than on public funds. The laws on private funds are detailed and precise in various aspects of fund operation. Investment trusts in Japan are under the regulation of the Financial Services Agency and the local agencies of the Ministry of Finance. The regulatory system and the registration process are rather complicated.

Comparison of the regulations

The discussion below will be on the regulations on the requirements for investors, the requirements for fund managers, operation, and information disclosure.

Entry threshold for investors

Table 5.1   Comparison of the official entry threshold for investors in various mature markets

United States	United Kingdom	Hong Kong	Japan
A bank, insurance company, registered investment company, business development company, or small business investment company; An employee benefit plan, within the meaning of the *Employee Retirement Income Security Act*, if a bank, insurance company, or registered investment adviser makes the investment decisions, or if the plan has total assets in excess of USD5 million;	An overseas individual; participant of unregulated collective investment schemes; investment professional; sophisticated investor; trust settlor, trustee, and personal representative; beneficiary of trust, will, or intestacy; An individual with an annual income exceeding GBP100,000 or net assets exceeding GBP250,000;	An authorized stock exchange, clearing house, controller, and other persons who provide automated trading services; An intermediary or a person who operates a business which provides investment service and is regulated by the laws of a location other than Hong Kong; An authorized financial institution, or bank regulated by the laws of a location other than Hong Kong;	"Qualified institutional investors" refers to the definitions in the Financial Instruments and Exchange Act: investors who have "expert knowledge of and experience with investment in securities." They include parties who are engaged in financial commodity exchange, banks, insurance companies, Shinkin banks and their association, labor banks and their association, the Norinchukin Bank, and the Shoko Chukin Bank.

Table 5.1   Comparison of the official entry threshold for investors in various mature markets

(Cont'd)

United States	United Kingdom	Hong Kong	Japan
A charitable organization, corporation, or partnership with assets exceeding USD5 million; A director, executive officer, or general partner of the company selling the securities; A business in which all the equity owners are accredited investors; A natural person who has individual net worth, or joint net worth with the person's spouse, that exceeds USD1 million at the time of the purchase, excluding the value of the primary residence of such a person; A natural person with income exceeding USD200,000 in each of the two most recent years or joint income with a spouse exceeding USD300,000 for those years and a reasonable expectation of the same income level in the current year; A trust with assets in excess of USD5 million, not formed to acquire the securities offered, whose purchases a sophisticated person makes.	A body corporate with more than 20 members with paid-in capital or net assets exceeding GBP500,000, or a company with paid-in capital or net assets exceeding GBP5 million; An unincorporated body or partnership enterprises with assets exceeding GBP5 million; A high-net-worth trust scheme.	An authorized insurer or a person who operates an insurance business and is regulated by the laws of a location other than Hong Kong; A person from a location other than Hong Kong.	Professional investors include qualified institutional investors, the state, and the Bank of Japan.

Note: The U.S. *Dodd-Frank Wall Street Reform and Consumer Protection Act* stipulates that the Government Accountability Office (GAO) was to conduct a study on qualified investors in order to evaluate the entry criteria of investors and submit the study to Congress.

Sources: The U.S. Securities and Exchange Commission, "Accredited Investors," http://www.sec.gov/answers/accred.htm; the U.K. *Financial Services and Markets Act*; Hong Kong's *Securities and Futures Ordinance*; and Japan's *Financial Instruments and Exchange Act* and *Financial Instruments and Exchange Act Enforcement Order*. Data analyzed by the Private Fund Research Center of Hua Ming Chuangfu Fund (HMC Fund).

The U.S. law on the requirements for qualified institutional and individual investors is the most detailed and clear. The U.K. law is less precise in comparison. The definitions of some terms are not provided. The Japan law is more rigorous but does not clearly define "private placement to general investors." The Hong Kong law is the most general. It does not address the asset threshold.

Entry threshold for managers

Table 5.2   Comparison of the official entry threshold for managers in various mature markets

United States	United Kingdom	Hong Kong	Japan
An investment advisor is required to register with the SEC.	—	A private fund manager shall possess relevant licenses in order to participate in securities and futures transactions.	A qualified investment trustee as defined in the Securities Investment Trust Law.

Sources: The U.S. Securities and Exchange Commission, "Accredited Investors," http://www.sec.gov/answers/accred.htm; the U.K. *Financial Services and Markets Act*; Hong Kong's *Securities and Futures Ordinance*; and *Japan's Financial Instruments and Exchange Act* and *Financial Instruments and Exchange Act Enforcement Order*. Data analyzed by the Private Fund Research Center of Hua Ming Chuangfu Fund (HMC Fund).

Since the establishment of private investment trusts, Japan has implemented rigorous examination of trust managers. After the 2008 global financial crisis, the U.S. has imposed stricter regulation over private funds. It stipulates the requirements for the registration of funds, despite the fact that exemption is granted to certain funds. The U.K. and Hong Kong have relatively slack regulations on the requirements for fund managers.

Operation

Table 5.3   Comparison of the operation requirements in various mature markets

United States	United Kingdom	Hong Kong	Japan
A private fund with capital exceeding USD150 million shall register with the SEC. A private fund with capital under USD100 million shall be regulated by the state government; a private fund with capital between USD100 million and USD150 million shall choose to register with the SEC or be regulated by the state government. A private fund shall safeguard and verify client assets by an independent public accountant.	—	—	A private investment trust shall submit the Securities Registration Statement and Securities Notice to the Ministry of Finance (Not applicable to private investment trusts offered to qualified institutional investors). An investment trust privately placed to general investors shall not be offered to more than 50 investors. Over 50% of the investments of a private investment trust shall be in securities

Sources: The U.S. Securities and Exchange Commission, "Accredited Investors," http://www.sec.gov/answers/accred.htm; the U.K. *Financial Services and Markets Act*; Hong Kong's *Securities and Futures Ordinance*; and Japan's *Financial Instruments and Exchange Act* and *Financial Instruments and Exchange Act Enforcement Order*. Data analyzed by the Private Fund Research Center of Hua Ming Chuangfu Fund (HMC Fund).

Japan and the U.S. have a more stringent regulation of the operation of private funds. The U.K. and Hong Kong's regulation of private funds remains relatively slack after the global financial crisis.

Information disclosure

Table 5.4   Comparison of the information disclosure requirements in various mature markets

United States	United Kingdom	Hong Kong	Japan
A private fund with assets exceeding USD150 million shall preserve data, reports, and studies on systemic risks, and provide such data to the SEC and the Financial Stability Oversight Council (FSOC). A venture capital fund is exempt from information disclosure. Family offices are exempt from registration and information disclosure. Information to disclose includes: total assets, leverage, transaction risks, trade and investment environment, valuation standards of the fund, assets class, and other information deemed essential by the SEC.	The FSA has the authority to request the manager or investors of a collective investment scheme which trade in the U.K. or is issued by a body corporate in the U.K. to provide relevant information.	—	The contract of a private investment trust shall include information on principal, profit allocation, evaluation of trust assets, and leverage and be submitted to the Prime Minister.

Sources: The U.S. Securities and Exchange Commission, "Accredited Investors," http://www.sec.gov/answers/accred.htm; the U.K. *Financial Services and Markets Act*; Hong Kong's *Securities and Futures Ordinance*; and Japan's *Financial Instruments and Exchange Act* and *Financial Instruments and Exchange Act Enforcement Order*. Data analyzed by the Private Fund Research Center of Hua Ming Chuangfu Fund (HMC Fund).

Japan depends on contact submission for initial regulation. The U.S. *Dodd-Frank Wall Street Reform and Consumer Protection Act* stipulates the responsibility and requirements of information disclosure of private funds, and the responsibilities of the regulators. It also establishes the administrative supervision as a legal possibility. The FSA of the U.K. requires collective investment schemes to provide transaction information, but the requirements are general. The execution of regulation may run into problems. Hong Kong does not impose regulations on information disclosure.

Lessons from mature markets

Regulatory system

From the cases of the U.S., the U.K., Hong Kong, and Japan, it is obvious that including private funds in the scope of regulation is a trend in the global financial industry. China should follow suit. Although Reform and Opening Up was launched and marketization began more than 30 years ago, China is still an emerging market and in economic transition. It has a lot to do to catch up with mature markets. The China financial market is lacking in penetration, breadth, and product diversity. Financial institutions are still developing and banks dominate the financial system. This poses the problem of asymmetrical information. Deception and price manipulation are common. Under such circumstances, there are bad influences in the privately offered fund industry. If it remains unregulated, the lemons problem may emerge. The bad institutions drive out the good ones, which leads to a market prolonged downturn. Therefore, regulation is essential for the long-term stable development of the privately offered funds.

At the same time, per capita income in China is rising. Households have an increasingly personalized and diverse demand for household wealth management. More privately offered funds are required to satisfy the demand. If the financial system fails to satisfy the demand, a huge amount of capital would flow to foreign markets. Foreign financial institutions are gaining a larger share of the China market than before. It has become more difficult for domestic financial institutions to expand their business, and the economic system is not safe or stable enough. Therefore, it is most important for China to support the development of privately offered funds and encourage financial innovation in order to maintain socioeconomic stability and development.

China should begin the legislation process of privately offered funds as soon as possible to reduce and avoid any risks induced by unregulated operation and to ensure the stability of the financial system. Mature markets have a relatively relaxed regulation of private funds under the premise that they do not pose a threat to financial stability. Private investments are guaranteed autonomy and privacy. China's privately offered funds are rapidly developing. China should allow market mechanisms to operate and should not implement unnecessary legal or administrative restrictions on privately offered funds. The state should provide a broad and independent legal platform for privately offered funds to develop. There should be a balance of rigorous regulation and flexibility so that privately offered funds can freely develop to a certain extent in an orderly manner.

Regulatory body

After 10 years of adopting the Forging Ahead Strategy, China's privately offered funds have grown to the size of more than RMB1 trillion. The fund industry is likely to continue to grow rapidly. China's privately offered funds are lacking in terms of size and number of products in comparison to the Western private funds which have a history of over 100 years. The regulation of private funds in developed countries operates in various modes. Taking into account future developments, China, as an emerging market in economic transition, should authorize only one regulatory body in order to effectively regulate and promote privately offered funds. At present, the China Securities Regulatory Commission (CSRC) is the most eligible institution.

Having a single regulator reduces transaction costs and raises efficiency in overseeing both financial products and financial institutions. The regulator would be able to encourage innovation at the same time. After the industry develops to a certain extent, China should consider a two-tier regulatory system similar to that of the U.S. Local regulators can shoulder some of the responsibilities of the central regulator in order to further improve efficiency.

Self-regulatory bodies

China should accelerate the founding of self-regulatory institutions of the privately offered fund industry. The industry should formulate its own rules and establish standards. The market should be allowed to perform self-regulation. In the past 10 years, national and local investment associates have been set up. However, associates of private securities investment are still in their infant stage. The Shenzhen Private Equity Association founded in March 2011 was the first private securities investment association in China.

Legal definition of privately offered funds

The definition of and name for private funds differ across countries. In China, "privately offered fund" is a broad and ambiguous concept. The law should provide a concrete and clear definition of "privately offered fund" and detail the scope and types of such funds.

Privately offered funds in China are not legally defined. They are understood in both a broad sense and a narrow sense. Sunshine private funds and private equity (PE) funds, two types of privately offered funds, are also referred to in both broad and narrow senses.

The lack of a clear legal definition hinders the development of privately offered funds. Only with a clear and precise definition of privately offered funds and their sub-categories can the funds be truly bound by law and develop under regulation to serve the market.

Entry threshold for investors

The scope and entry thresholds for investors should be clearly defined to ensure that the investors have certain risk resistance capacity. This acts as a safety barrier.

Entry threshold for managers

The rapid development of China's privately offered funds is in need of legislation which requires privately offered funds to register and have clear regulations on managers and management. These regulations would prevent misbehavior or chaos in the industry. At the same time, China should issue guidelines or directives on the internal regulation of privately offered funds, including the fundraising process, decision-making process regarding investments, and risk control system. It would help privately offered funds build reputation and protect the investors' interests.

Requirements for information disclosure

As the size and the number of privately offered funds grow, the funds will inevitably have a strong impact on the stability of China's financial system. Therefore, requirements in information disclosure should be strict. We recommend that the regulatory body make it a requirement for privately offered funds to provide information on the size of the fund, asset class, financial derivatives, valuation of the fund, and operation.

Regulations on internal risk control and investment operations should be implemented in order to avert principal-agent risks. "Rat trading" and other violations should be curbed to protect the investors' interests.

Environment for the Regulation of Investment Funds in China

In this section, we start off with an introduction to the history of the regulatory system of public funds in China as a reference for the study of the current regulatory system. We will then analyze the environment for the regulation of privately offered funds.

Regulatory system of public funds in China

Evolution of the regulatory system of public funds

As of the end of 2010, there were 62 public fund management companies in China, managing 714 public funds, with total assets under management (AUM) of RMB2.5 trillion. The AUM expanded to RMB3.3 trillion in 2007. Public funds have become a major force in the capital market in China. The evolution of their regulatory system can be divided into three phases.

Old funds and the lack of unified regulation (1991–1997)

The opening of the Shanghai Stock Exchange and the Shenzhen Stock Exchange signified the opening of the securities market in China. The first group of investment funds in China emerged in 1991. In October, Wuhan Securities Investment Fund and Shenzhen Nanshan Venture Capital Fund were established with the approval from the People's Bank of China and the government of the Nanshan District in Shenzhen, respectively. In the following year, 57 funds were launched. The number hit a record high. The Agricultural Bank of China Shenyang Trust & Investment Company became listed on the Shenyang Stock Exchange and began issuing beneficiary certification. It was the first beneficiary certification that could be traded over-the-counter. The Shenzhen Investment Fund Management Company was founded with the approval from the local government and it launched the largest domestic fund at that time, the Tianji Fund, which held RMB581 million in assets. On November 11, 1992, with approval from the People's Bank of China, the Zibo Town & Township Investment Funds Corp., Ltd., was founded by five financial institutions, including the Agricultural Development Bank Trust & Investment Company. It was the first authoritative and regulated corporate contract type fund. It raised RMB300 million and had a duration of eight years. On August 20, 1993, Zibo Town & Township Investment Funds became listed on the Shanghai Stock Exchange. It was the first investment fund which was traded on the stock exchange. In early 1993, Jianye, Jinlong, and Baoding Education Funds were launched in Shanghai with the approval from the People's Bank of China. They assembled RMB300 million in capital and became listed on the Shanghai Stock Exchange at the end of the year. These funds were called "old funds." It was an exploratory and experimental period in China's investment funds. The experience was valuable for later when the regulated securities investment funds developed. As of October 1997, there were 72 investment funds in China. They raised RMB6.6 billion in total.[8]

The regulation of investment funds launched during 1991–1997 was chaotic. The funds were granted approval by different bodies, including the headquarters and local branches of the People's Bank of China, and the local governments. There was a lack of standardized regulations. Approvals were granted according to the local regulations, such as the *Shenzhen Interim Provisions on the Administration of Investment Trust* and *Shanghai Measures for the Administration of Renminbi Securities Investment Trust*. There was no standardized regulation or recognized regulatory body to effectively regulate the establishment and management of the funds. The operation of funds was under no supervision. Some funds acted as the manager, trustee, and promoter at the same time. Some of the funds even did not have a trustee.

In the early development of China's investment funds during 1991–1992, the funds were mainly supervised by the People's Bank of China, which was assisted by multiple bodies such as the State Council and local governments. These different bodies supervised the funds according to their own rules. In October 1992, the State Council Securities Commission (SCSC) and the China Securities Regulatory Commission (CSRC) were established. The regulatory system was greatly improved. The *Notice of the State Council Concerning Further Strengthening Macro-Administration of the Securities Market* announced in December 1992 stipulated the duties of the CSRC, the SCSC, the People's Bank of China, the Ministry of Finance, the State Commission for Restructuring the Economic System, and the local governments in the regulation of the securities markets. Despite having the CSRC and SCSC as the major regulators, there were still too many regulatory bodies. In April 1998, according to the reform agenda of the State Council, the SCSC was integrated into the CSRC. The CSRC then came directly under the State Council.

New funds and unified regulation (1997–2004)

On June 14, 1997, the *Interim Measures for the Management of Securities Investment Funds*, the first national regulation on securities investment, was announced. It was one of the milestones of China's investment funds and the regulatory system. It signified the unified regulation of public funds in China. The *Interim Measures for the Management of Securities Investment Funds* and its associated implementation guidelines, and the *Pilot Scheme of Open-End Securities Investment Funds* became the core of the regulatory system. There were around 50 regulations which were related to the launching, operation, information disclosure, practitioners, and access of funds.

Shortly after the announcement of the *Interim Measures for the Management of Securities Investment Funds*, the CSRC issued the *Notice on Several Issues Concerning Applications for the Establishment of Fund Management Companies* and the *Notice of Relevant Issues Concerning Approval of Securities Investment Funds*. In March 1998, the first two regulated securities investment fund companies — Guotai Asset Management Co., Ltd., and China Southern Asset Management Co., Ltd. — were founded. The first close-end securities investment funds — Kaiyuan Fund and Jintai Fund — were launched. These regulated funds were called "new funds."

On October 8, 2000, the CSRC announced the *Pilot Scheme of Open-End Securities Investment Funds*. Open-end funds came officially under the regulation of the CSRC. About a year later, the first open-end fund in China — HuaAn Fund — was launched. It was a major innovation of the fund industry.

In this phase, China's regulatory system began to take shape. The CSRC was appointed to be the highest authority in fund regulation. In October 1997, the Department of Fund Supervision of the CSRC began operation. In August 2001, the self-regulatory institution — Chinese Association of Securities Investment Funds — was established. In December 2004, the Securities Investment Fund Industry Committee of the Securities Association of China (SAC) was founded. It acted as a discussion platform for professionals who were engaged in the industry. It took over from the Chinese Association of Securities Investment Funds. The Committee was renamed as Securities Investment Fund Industry Professional Committee in 2007. In the same year, the SAC set up a membership department, which was responsible for monitoring the member fund management companies and custodian banks.

Compared to the time when the old funds were launched without unified regulation, during 1997–2004, there were prominent improvements and breakthroughs. The organizational framework of the regulation of the fund industry had been established and the responsibilities of each organization well-defined. It rectified the problems and strengthened the system. The gradual exploration and implementation of regulations provided legal protection to the fund industry in terms of the corporate governance structure, independence of custodians, and information disclosure. This laid the path for the legislation process of securities investment funds. Under an improved regulatory system, the fund industry expanded rapidly. As of the end of 2003, there were 26 fund management companies, managing 114 securities investment fund products with a total AUM of RMB168.1 billion.[9]

The fund industry of China has a relatively short history. Despite the fact that the regulatory system had been reinforced, there were many loopholes. In October 2000, *Caijing Magazine* published an article titled "Inside Story of Funds: An Analysis of the Behaviors of Funds" which shocked the entire industry and the public. It sparked debate about the industry. The article analyzed the transaction records of 22 securities investment funds managed by 10 fund management companies from August 9, 1999 to April 28, 2000. It exposed the violations committed by the companies and that market manipulation was a common practice. This raised the questions of whether investment funds, as institutional investors, could stabilize the market and whether fund managers had their clients' interests in mind. The loopholes and problems of the regulatory system at that time were apparent.

Legal regulation of funds (2004–present)

The National People's Congress passed the *Law on Securities Investment Fund* in October 2003 which signified the beginning of the legal regulation of investment funds in China. The Law came into effect on June 1, 2004.

The implementation of the *Law on Securities Investment Fund* granted the fund industry legal status. The industry entered into a new stage. This created room for development for the industry and offered better regulation of the operation of funds. The *Interim Measures for the Management of Securities Investment Funds* was annulled in August 2004 with approval from the State Council.

Regulatory system of public funds

Goals and principles

The International Organization of Securities Commissions (IOSCO)'s 1998 *Objectives and Principles of Securities Regulation* states three objectives of securities regulation[10]:

- The protection of investors;
- Ensuring that markets are fair, efficient, and transparent;
- The reduction of systemic risk.

These three objectives are applicable to China.[11] Taking into account the fact that the capital market of China is emerging and is in transition, the regulation of securities investment funds also shoulders the responsibility to promote the fund industry. The objectives of the regulation of securities investments can be summarized as follows:

(1) Protection of investors

The protection of investors' interests is the primary goal of the regulation of funds. Investors are the fundraising channel for the fund industry. The industry would collapse without the capital. Investors suffer from asymmetric information in the operation of funds. Therefore, the regulation of funds should revolve around the protection of investors.

(2) Ensuring market fairness, efficiency, and transparency

The regulator and regulatory policies should establish an efficient, transparent, and fair market system in order to curb illegal behaviors such as deception, market manipulation, and insider trading.

(3) Reduction of systemic risk

The regulatory bodies should implement preventive measures to minimize systemic risk such as a market entry threshold to maintain stability in the market.

(4) Promotion of regulation of the fund industry

China's investment fund industry is small and developing. The regulatory bodies should strike a balance between regulation and promotion.

China's regulation of funds follows the following six principles:

(1) Legal regulation

A legal regulatory system should be established.

(2) Open, fair, and just

The regulatory bodies should be open so that information is transparent. It should ensure that the market participants enjoy equal rights. It should treat the entities under its regulation with justice.

(3) Value both regulation and self-regulation

Other than legislation and administrative measures, the regulatory bodies should emphasize the value of self-regulation of the industry. Self-regulatory organizations should be established and self-regulation should be encouraged.

(4) Continuous and effective regulation

The regulatory bodies should devise policies which can be continuously applied in order to ensure the orderly development of the industry and prevent fluctuations. These policies should also be cost-effective.

(5) Prudential regulation

Investment funds are collective investment vehicles. Investments in securities such as stocks and financial derivatives incur high risks. The regulatory body should be prudent when setting the market entry threshold and overseeing the operation of funds. It should take future risks into account.

(6) Balance between regulation and development
The regulatory bodies should regulate the industry while also helping to promote the industry.

Regulatory bodies and their functions

At present, the CSRC is the core of the unified regulatory system. Other regulatory bodies include the regional offices of the CSRC, custodian banks, stock exchanges, and self-regulatory organizations.

(1) The China Securities Regulatory Commission and its regional offices
The CSRC, as the principal regulatory body in China's fund industry, regulates the fund market and participates according to the law. In order to exercise the full advantage of a unified regulatory system, the CSRC authorized regional offices to work on the frontline. The Department of Fund Supervision was in charge of the regulation of funds, which mainly relies on the market entry threshold and continuous supervision. Its main functions include:
- Devise major policies related to the fund industry;
- Draft regulations and the details for implementation;
- Examine the administrative licensing items of funds;
- Supervise fund management companies, fund trustees, and fund sales;
- Verify the qualifications of the senior management personnel in the fund industry and oversee their business operations;
- Direct and coordinate the daily supervision of funds by the regional CSRC offices and stock exchanges;
- Direct and oversee the fund industry associations; and
- Handle major problems with daily supervision.

(2) Securities Association of China
The SAC is a non-profit-making corporate social group. It is a self-regulatory body formed by financial institutions which are engaged in the securities business. Self-regulation is conducted in the following ways:
- Set up rules and business standards;
- Regulate members and other practitioners;
- Educate members to abide by the law and administrative regulations;
- Defend the legal rights of the members;

- Set up industry practitioner examinations and the education system in order to improve the quality of practitioners;
- Facilitate communications among members and across countries; and
- Encourage the industry to build reputation.

The membership department of the CSRC is responsible for the following:
- Monitor the member fund management companies and custodian banks;
- Educate member companies to abide by the law and administrative regulations;
- Set up and oversee the implementation of self-regulatory rules and business standards;
- Assist the SAC;
- Encourage member companies to build reputation and information management;
- Defend the legal rights of the members and reflect on the opinions of the members;
- Prepare statistics of the fund industry;
- Shadow pricing and securities valuation;
- Handle complaints about the member companies and mediate in disputes; and
- Coordinate member companies in the launching of investors' education.

(3) Stock exchanges

Stock exchanges regulate the listing and information disclosure of funds and oversee the transactions of funds on the stock exchanges.

(4) Fund custodians

A fund custodian is the keeper of the fund assets. It is one of the regulators of funds. A custodian is independent of the fund manager. The custodian safeguards and audits the fund assets and oversees the operation of the fund as stated in the contract. It opens an independent account for the fund and ensures that the fund manager abides by the contract and fund regulations to protect the rights of the investors.

(5) Other organizations

Other regulatory bodies include the People's Bank of China and the China Banking Regulatory Commission. They perform their duties as stipulated in the law and administrative regulations. They supervise the operation of funds.

Legal system and the main content of regulation

In June 2004, after the *Law on Securities Investment Fund* had been implemented, China established a legal regulatory system of the fund industry based on the *Law* and its eight supporting regulations. There were supplementary departmental regulations and documents, and also self-regulatory regulations. The main content of the CSRC's regulation of funds includes the following:

(1) Market entry threshold
The CSRC authorizes the operation of fund management companies, custodian banks, and fund sales institutions, and the entry of institutions serving the funds into the market.

(2) Continuous daily supervision
The CSRC conducts on- and off-site inspection to monitor the operation of fund management companies, custodian banks, and fund sales institutions. It supervises the internal management and operation of institutions serving the funds on a daily basis.

(3) Regulation of fund operation
Regulation focuses on the approval of the offerings of funds, fund sales activities, information disclosure, and the investment and transaction behavior of the funds.

(4) Supervision of senior management personnel and investment managers
The CSRC imposes requirements on the qualifications of senior management personnel and investment managers in the fund industry.

Regulatory system of privately offered funds in China

China's securities investment funds develop as the securities markets grow. There are privately offered funds in all securities markets. The development of privately offered funds is a natural and essential outcome of market development as a response to the investors' demand. Since their emergence, privately offered funds have experienced the initial development, adjustment, "sunshine" exploration, and rapid development stages. Their organization, size, market influence, and investment philosophy have changed. Privately offered funds began as a gentlemen's agreement but have evolved into corporate type funds, and later limited partnership funds and trust funds. Their operation is becoming more diverse and regulated. The size of funds is expanding. However, due to the higher growth rate of the capital market, the proportion of privately offered funds to total market size is decreasing. The influence of privately offered funds is weakening.

As China's securities market and its participants (e.g., regulators, service agencies, and investors) begin to mature, the structure of privately offered fund managers and their investment philosophy changed. A "privately offered fund" was no longer a euphemism for "market manipulation" and "insider trading."

Some financial practitioners who have had professional training enter into the profession of fund managers. They followed the modern portfolio theory and the philosophy of value investing. They became one of the factors which promotes market maturation and stability. In 2004, Zhao Danyang and the Shenzhen International Trust & Investment Co., Ltd. (SZITIC) launched the first securities investment trust in China — SZITIC Pure Heart China Investment Trust. It signified that privately offered funds had entered into a "sunshine" period after a period of chaos. Privately offered fund managers acted as "investment consultants." In the seven years that followed, trust type privately offered funds developed rapidly. Sunshine private funds were expanding quickly. During this "sunshine" period, the public began to understand the operation of privately offered funds. The funds gained greater acceptance and recognition.

Although the emergence of privately offered funds is formidable and inevitable, and the funds are becoming more organized and regulated, they failed to obtain legal status. The funds exist in the grey area. When the *Law on Fund* was formulated around 2003, the regulatory authorities had been keeping an eye on the continuously growing privately offered funds. However, taking into account the fact that multiple regulatory bodies including the CSRC, China Banking Regulatory Commission (CBRC), National Development and Reform Commission, and the Ministry of Finance needed to be involved, and coordination would be difficult, the content about "privately offered funds" was omitted when the draft was submitted to the Financial and Economic Affairs Committee of the National People's Congress. The law was amended to be the *Law on Securities Investment Fund*. Article 2 stipulatesthe following[12]: This Law is applicable to the raising of capital for investment in securities by openly selling fund units within the territory of the People's Republic of China (hereinafter referred to as funds, for short), which are managed by fund managers, placed in the custody of fund custodians, and used, in the interest of the holders of fund units, for investment in securities in the form of portfolios. With respect to matters which are not covered by the provisions of this Law, the provisions of the *Trust Law of the People's Republic of China*, the *Securities Law of the People's Republic of China*, and other relevant laws and administrative regulations shall apply.

This excluded privately offered funds from the *Law on Securities Investment Fund*. As of the time of this writing, privately offered funds have not been granted legal status.[13]

Private securities investment funds can be categorized into "sunshine" and underground funds. The underground funds are unregulated and not bound by the law. The government has made it clear that it is against underground funds and considers them a form of illegal fundraising and a disruption of the financial industry. The scale of underground funds is large. The liabilities of the parties involved are undefined and not legally bound. Being unregulated, the transactions of underground funds may be in violation of the laws and regulations of the financial and securities markets. Because of the hidden and flexible nature of underground funds, the regulation of such funds is difficult. Under the current situation, it would be a better choice to transform underground funds into sunshine private funds. However, sunshine private funds should be legalized first. This would put underground private funds under legal regulation.

Sunshine private funds are a financial innovation in the privately offered fund industry. They emerged as products of the attempt of privately offered funds to obtain market recognition and achieve institutional breakthrough. Sunshine private funds are partially regulated. The biggest contribution of sunshine private funds was to incorporate the trusteeship system into privately offered funds. The trust assets are safeguarded by an independent, third-party, custodian bank. It is to ensure the safety of the clients' assets. As trust type sunshine private funds are collective trust funds issued by trust companies, they are essentially trusts. The government department which regulates trust companies is the CBRC. In a way, the CBRC has become the major regulator of trust type sunshine private funds, and the funds need to report to the CBRC or its regional offices after they are launched. However, such funds mainly invest in the stocks and bonds in the secondary market. There is a mismatch between the regulators and the operation of trust type sunshine private funds.

The launching and operation of trust type sunshine private funds are bound by the *Trust Law* and *Measures for the Administration of Trust Companies' Trust Plans of Assembled Funds* announced by the Standing Committee of the National People's Congress. The latter document stipulates the role of trust companies as trustees and privately offered fund companies as investment consultants. It also provides detailed regulations on collective trust funds launched by trust companies, including the requirements for qualified investors, the number of investors, trust period, investment direction, and restrictions, and information disclosure. The regulations are applicable to sunshine private funds[14]:

- A "qualified investor" shall meet the following requirements:
  (i) a natural person, legal person, or an organization established according to law, whose minimum investment in a trust plan is RMB1 million or more;
  (ii) a natural person whose total individual or family financial assets exceed RMB1 million at the time when he/she subscribes to the trust plan and who can provide the relevant property certificate;
  (iii) a natural person whose annual income exceeds RMB200,000 for the latest three years or whose annual income plus the annual income of his/her spouse exceeds RMB300,000 for the latest three years and who can provide the relevant income certificate.
- The trust period shall be one year or more.
- There are clear investment orientation and investment strategies for the trust capital, which shall also be in line with the industrial policies of the state and other relevant provisions.
- A trust company shall not provide guarantees for any other person; the loans it provides to any other person shall not exceed 30% of the paid-in balance of all the trust plans subject to its management.
- The trust contract shall prescribe the remuneration for the trustee. Except for fair remunerations, the trust company shall not seek any profit for itself or anyone else either directly or indirectly by using the trust properties under any name.
- A trust company shall not undertake any transaction between the inherent properties and trust properties.

Detailed requirements for information disclosure, custody of assets, and promotion are also stipulated in the *Measures for the Administration of Trust Companies' Trust Plans of Assembled Funds*. The CBRC also announced the *Operating Guidelines for the Securities Investment Trust Business of Trust Companies*. It stipulates that the third-party investment consultant shall meet the following conditions:

- A company or limited partnership company established by law without records of major violations;
- Have paid-in capital of over RMB10 million;
- Have a qualified securities investment management and research team; members shall pass the Licensing Examination for Securities Intermediaries, have three years of experience, good reputation, and traceable proof of securities management records, and without records of violations;

- Have a well-established business management and risk control system; have a regulated background management system and operation procedures;
- Have a fixed place of business and suitable hardware and software facilities;
- Not related to the trust company in any way; and
- Other requirements of the CBRC.

Trust type sunshine private funds are regulated to a certain extent. There is an entry threshold for investors and investment consultants, as well as requirements for operational management and information disclosure. The regulation is essential for the protection of investors and their assets. Trust type sunshine private funds are the most regulated form of private securities investment funds. They have been developing quickly since their first emergence. They have become an important investment vehicle for high-end customers and the HNWIs.

Despite rapid development and obtaining market recognition, the market remains dubious about the regulation of trust type sunshine private funds.

Sunshine private funds have not been granted legal status yet. The funds are not regulated by the law. This is the biggest impediment to the development of the industry. In early 2011, the *Chinese Securities Journal* sent out questionnaires to 41 sunshine private funds and 22 responded, of which 17 supported the legislation of the funds and hoped to obtain legal status.[15]

The regulators and the operation of sunshine private funds are not entirely compatible, and the regulators do not support the funds. At present, there is not a consensus on the definition or the understanding of "private offering." The CSRC and the CBRC have separate regulations for and different beliefs in regulating the operation of the market. There are many issues with the operation and regulation of sunshine private funds which have to be dealt with. In July 2009, China Securities Depository and Clearing Co., Ltd (CSDCC), which is under the authority of the CSRC, suspended trust companies from opening shareholder accounts. Many trust companies were therefore unable to launch new investment trust products. The CSRC claimed that its interference was a response to trust companies opening a large number of accounts to speculate against IPO shares. Another reading of the interference was that the CSRC was making way for the segregated account management products of the public funds under its regulation. Apart from not having an authorized regulator, this also shows that regulatory bodies have not granted their approval of sunshine private funds.

The lack of a regulatory system significantly hinders the development of sunshine private funds. Places with a developed private fund industry are equipped with a comprehensive regulatory system. The method and scope of regulation, the regulators, and laws and regulations are well defined.

As the privately offered fund industry continues to develop, China has an urgent need to establish a comprehensive regulatory system. This can be achieved by learning from the experience of mature markets and China's own public funds and tailoring the system to its unique financial market, taking it into the developmental stage of the privately offered funds. Appropriate regulation of the funds would guide the development of the funds, encourage favorable development of the financial market, and maintain market stability.

6
Chapter

Analysis of the Development of China's Privately Offered Fund Industry

In February 2004, the Shenzhen International Trust and Investment Co., Ltd. (SZITIC, now China Resource SZITIC Trust Co., Ltd.), launched the SZITIC Pure Heart China Investment Trust. It led China's private securities investment funds onto the road of regulation. By 2011, after eight years of development, there have been more than 1,000 such products in the market. The prospects for sunshine private funds are promising. Since 2007, the performances of private securities investment funds have been impressive. The domestic demand for private securities investment fund products began to grow rapidly. The number of new products continued to increase dramatically and the assets under management by the products expanded.

Most of the data presented in this chapter are from sunshine private funds of privately offered fund management companies and trust companies. This is because sunshine private funds are the only privately securities investment funds which have data available and they are becoming the preferred form of private securities investment funds.

Launch of Sunshine Private Funds in the Past

It was 2007 when sunshine private funds first entered into the period of rapid development. The compound annual growth rate of the launch of new products for 2007–2010 was as high as 57%. In 2007 alone, 141 new sunshine private funds were launched, which was more than the sum of the number of products launched in the previous four years. In 2008, despite the impact of the global financial crisis, more than 160 products were launched.

In 2009, the growth of sunshine private funds was explosive. Some 397 products were launched and 73 were issued in June alone. In the second half of the year, the number of products launched dropped. During that time, some trust companies opened a large number of "tractor accounts"[1] in order to increase the success rate. This caused the regulatory bodies to suspend trust companies from opening securities investment accounts. Some new fund waiting for placement failed to launch. As there were increasingly few securities investment accounts in the market, the trust companies' securities investment accounts became more valuable. With few securities investment opened before suspension. Trust companies reserved those accounts for privately offered fund companies which had a better business performance and market recognition. This satisfied the demand of some privately offered funds to expand, but more such funds were suppressed. In 2010, crisis hit China's economy. The A-share market suffered a sharp shock. The differentiation between large- and small-cap shares was serious. The structural opportunities of the market for privately offered funds were unprecedented. In that year, 549 sunshine private funds were launched, a 38% growth from the previous year. They contributed to 43% of the total number of funds launched during 2004–2010. The number of sunshine private funds launched in each year is shown in Fig. 6.1.

Fig. 6.1 Number of sunshine private funds launched, 2004–first half of 2011

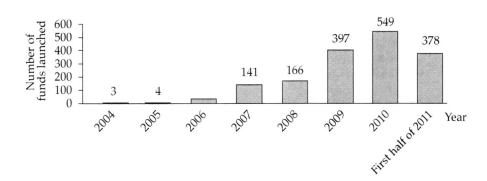

Note: Funds without an investment manager or whose investment manager is a securities company, public fund, or a bank are excluded.

Source: Data from Wind Info analyzed by the Private Fund Research Center of Hua Ming Chuangfu Fund (HMC Fund).

The issue size of sunshine private funds is minute compared to that of public funds which can amount to a few billion shares. Sunshine private funds are restricted to having not more than 50 investors, and their issue size is usually around a RMB10 million. Once the investment capability of privately offered fund companies is recognized in the market, investors would make additional investment. The subsequent growth rate of asset size should not be underestimated. In recent years, in terms of the number of new fund products launched, the growth of public funds is not as strong as the growth of privately offered funds (See Fig. 6.2).

As of the end of May 2011, there were 1,379 sunshine private funds.[2] Based on the estimation that each fund raise RMB100 million, the size of sunshine private funds amounted to RMB150 billion, 6% of the size of public funds.

Fig. 6.2   Number of public and privately offered funds launched, 2004–2010

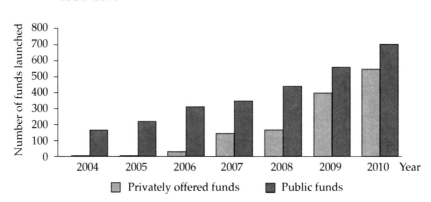

Source: Data from Wind Info analyzed by the Private Fund Research Center of Hua Ming Chuangfu Fund (HMC Fund).

Globally, as of the end of 2010, there were 9,550 hedge funds with a total asset size of USD1.9 trillion, which was one-twelfth of that of global mutual funds. In the U.S. market where hedge funds are the most developed, the size of hedge funds is around one-ninth of that of mutual funds (See Fig. 6.3). In Japan's market, which is similar to the China market, the size of private funds is around half of that of public funds. It can be deduced that the room for sunshine private funds to develop is huge.

Fig. 6.3   Size of the U.S. hedge funds, 2001–2010

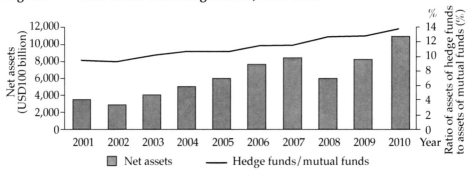

Source: Morningstar, http://www.morningstar.com.

Sunshine private fund practitioners and researchers

As sunshine private funds develop, the demand of privately offered funds companies for financial practitioners who specialize in sunshine private funds increases. They require a better team of managers and researchers. According to

Simuwang's *Report on China's Private Securities Funds for the First Six Months of 2011*, 57.58% privately offered funds had 10 to 20 employees. There were few large companies (See Fig. 6.4). The number of employees of public fund companies is shown in Fig.6.5.

Fig. 6.4   Number of employees of privately offered fund companies

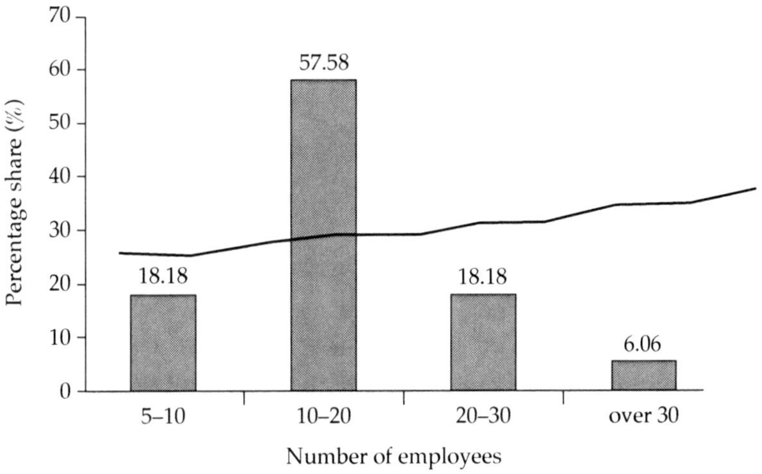

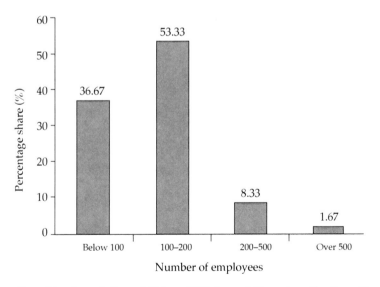

Source: Simuwang, *Report on China's Private Securities Funds for the First Six Months of 2011*.

Fig. 6.5   Number of employees of public fund companies

Source: Securities Association of China, *2009 Annual Report on the Securities Investment Fund Industry in China*.

According to the *2009 Annual Report on the Securities Investment Fund Industry in China* published by the Securities Association of China, as of the end of 2009, the 60 public fund companies in China employed 8,055 persons, 10 times that of sunshine private fund companies. Despite the huge difference of the number of employees, the operation of the two types of funds is similar. The organization and structure of sunshine private funds is being refined. It is natural for the funds to hire more financial practitioners.

In the fund industry, the investment research team is the most important human resources to the fund company, and the fund managers are the "soul" of the company.

Half of the private fund management companies only had one fund manager, about a quarter employed two to three managers, and only 18.18% employed more than three managers (See Fig. 6.6).

For public funds, as of the end of 2009, 60 companies employed 482 managers, on average 8 managers per company.

Fig. 6.6 **Number of managers privately offered fund companies employed**

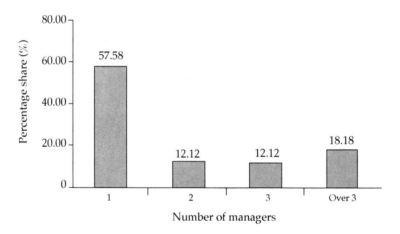

Source: Simuwang, *Report on China's Private Securities Funds for the First Six Months of 2011.*

As for the research team, 61% of privately offered fund companies had a team of 5 to 10 researchers. Only 9% employed more than 10 researchers (See Fig. 6.7). The researchers normally have over 10 years of experience in the securities business. They are experienced in securities investments or relevant fields such as private equity (PE).

Fig. 6.7   **Number of researchers privately offered fund companies employed**

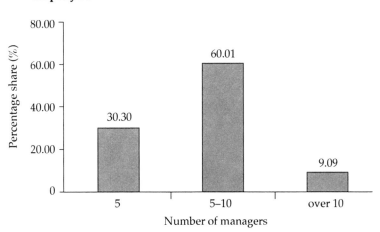

Source: Simuwang, *Report on China's Private Securities Funds for the First Six Months of 2011.*

Judging by the current rate of expansion of sunshine private funds, it is natural that more financial practitioners will be employed as privately offered fund managers. In recent years, it is not uncommon for public fund managers to turn to privately offered funds. The incentive mechanism of sunshine private funds is effective as the performance of a manager is tied to the business performance of the fund. In addition, the operation of privately offered fund is flexible and less tightly regulated. The funds are not required to release information on their net assets or investment records every day. The managers are less stressed. Flexibility and the incentive mechanism are what attract many top fund managers.

Features of the geographical distribution of privately offered fund companies

As of the end of May 2011, according to statistics, there were 446 privately offered fund companies in China. 2007 was the year in which most such companies were established (66). Based on the location of registration, it can be seen that most companies were based in the Yangtze River Delta economic zone, Pearl River Delta economic zone, and the Beijing-Tianjin region. The geographical distribution is similar to that of public funds (See Fig. 6.8 and Fig. 6.9). The Yangtze River Delta economic zone was the area with the most companies (184, 41%). The companies in that area were concentrated in Shanghai. The Pearl River Delta economic zone had the second most companies

(28%) with companies concentrating in Shenzhen. Companies in the Beijing-Tianjin region, and other locations took up 21% and 10%, respectively, of the total number of companies.

Fig. 6.8   Geographical distribution of privately offered fund companies

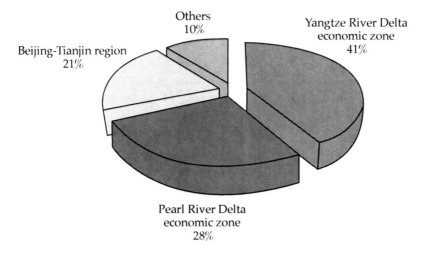

Source: Data from Wind Info analyzed by the Private Fund Research Center of Hua Ming Chuangfu Fund (HMC Fund).

Fig. 6.9   Geographical distribution of public fund companies

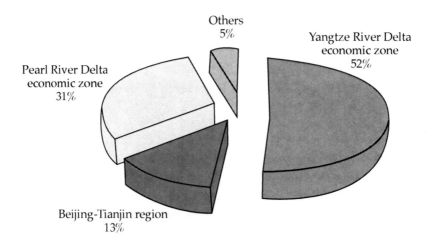

Source: Data from Wind Info analyzed by the Private Fund Research Center of Hua Ming Chuangfu Fund (HMC Fund).

The geographical distribution of privately offered fund products is similar to that of the privately offered fund companies. The reasons behind that are as follows:

- There are a large number of high-net-worth individuals (HNWIs) and therefore a great demand for wealth management products in the region.
- The regional economy is large and active.
- There are many financial institutions and practitioners in the region; the financial market is favorable.
- The region assumes political advantage.

Great number of high-net-worth individuals and huge demand for wealth management products

According to Forbes and the China Construction Bank's *China Private Wealth Report 2010*, 53% of China's HNWIs and more than 70% of ultra-high-net-worth individuals (UNWIs) resided in Guangdong Province, Zhejiang Province, Jiangsu Province, Beijing, and Shanghai. There were almost 80,000 HNWIs in Guangdong Province, followed by 40,000 in Zhejiang Province. Both Beijing and Shanghai host approximately 27,000 HNWIs each (See Fig. 6.10).

Fig. 6.10   Top 10 locations with the greatest number of high-net-worth individuals

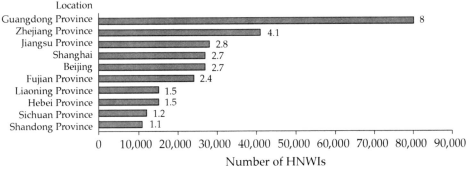

Source: Data from Forbes and the China Construction Bank's *China Private Wealth Report 2010*.

The HNWIs in Beijing, Shanghai, and Guangdong Province differ from those in other locations. They do not have as strong a preference for cash or savings. With higher risk-bearing abilities, they prefer alternative investments and have a greater demand for differentiated, personalized wealth management products. The investment strategies of sunshine private funds offer flexibility, which caters to the needs of refined asset management of HNWIs. This is why the demand for sunshine private fund products is higher in those locations.

Large regional economy and high degree of economic activity

A favorable economic environment is a prerequisite for financial development. Economic prosperity and high degree of economic activity is an advantage of Shanghai, Shenzhen, Beijing, and Tianjin. Based on the ranking of regional GDP in 2009, Shanghai was ranked first with RMB1.49 trillion, followed by Beijing, Guangzhou, Shenzhen, and Tianjin (See Fig. 6.11). The GDP per capita and GDP growth rate were high. Tianjin attained a 16% growth rate which topped the list. These regions with favorable conditions are attractive to privately offered fund companies.

A similar trend is noticed in the global private fund industry. In Europe and the U.S. where financial markets are the most active, the size of private funds is much larger than that in other countries or regions.

Fig. 6.11 Top 10 cities based on regional GDP

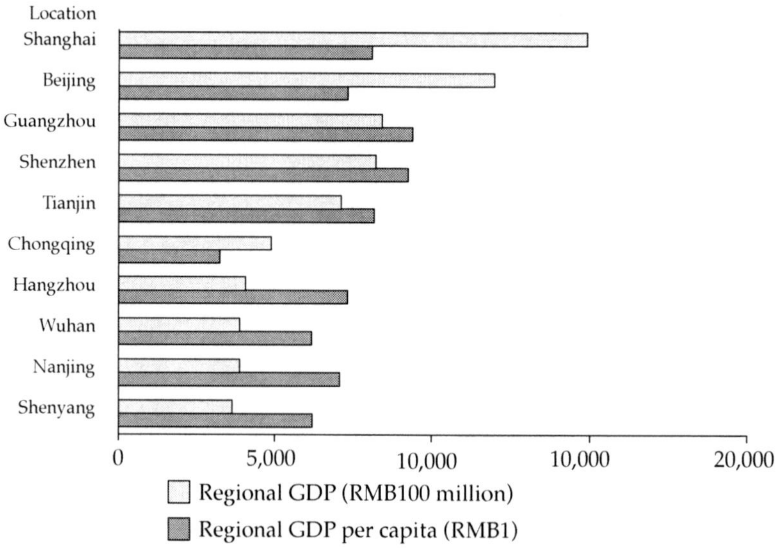

Source: China Economic Information Network, http://db.cei.gov.cn.

Great number of talents in financial institutions and favorable financial environment

A great pool of financial talents and a favorable financial environment are characteristics of the locations where privately offered fund companies concentrate. These factors imply a favorable investment environment and high sensitivity to the market. Companies would be able to grasps better investment opportunities.

Shanghai and Shenzhen attract a lot of financial institutions thanks to the Shanghai Stock Exchange and Shenzhen Stock Exchange. As of the end of 2009, there were 787 financial institutions and 170 foreign operating financial institutions in Shanghai.[3] The advantages in the hard environment are prominent. The establishment of financial infrastructure is especially fast in the Lujiazui Central Business District. The district has attracted a lot of talents and financial activity is high.

The financial development and benefits of Shenzhen have improved thanks to government support policies. As of the end of 2010, Shenzhen was host to the headquarters of 78 financial institutions. The cooperation between Shenzhen and Hong Kong also propels the financial development and innovation in Shenzhen. The financial industry in Shenzhen is comparable in terms of the system, mechanisms, philosophy, techniques, talents, and products to the financial industries in Hong Kong, Macau, Taiwan, and around the globe.

The advantage of Beijing is that it is where regulatory institutions are based. Financial institutions there have greater access to information and are more sensitive to policies. They are more able to foresee the macroeconomic policy trends. In addition, Beijing is also home to a lot of tertiary institutions. The supply of financial talents is abundant. This is important for an industry which relies on human resources. This guarantees the development potential for the financial industry in Beijing.

The advantage of Tianjin lies in its preferential policies. Its recent rapid development in the financial industry cannot be neglected. CEIBS Lujiazui International Finance Research Center's *Theoretical Framework for the Evaluation and Comparison of Chinese Cities' Financial Development* released in 2010 evaluates the level of development of various cities in terms of the ability to gather funds, financial risk management, degree of financial deepening, diversity of financial institutions, and diversity of financial products. The analysis showed that the top four cities were Beijing, Shanghai, Shenzhen, and Guangzhou (See Table 6.1). Based on *Xinhua-Dow Jones International Financial Centers Development Index (2011)*, in the comprehensive evaluation of international financial centers, Shanghai, Beijing, and Shenzhen were ranked 6th, 14th, and 21st, respectively.

Table 6.1   Comprehensive evaluation of international financial centers in China

Rank	City	Score	Rank	City	Score
1	Beijing	0.82	6	Nanjing	0.30
2	Shanghai	0.75	7	Chengdu	0.29
3	Shenzhen	0.51	8	Suzhou	0.29
4	Guangzhou	0.33	9	Chongqing	0.27
5	Hangzhou	0.31	10	Tianjin	0.26

Source: CEIBS Lujiazui International Finance Research Center, *Theoretical Framework for the Evaluation and Comparison of Chinese Cities' Financial Development (2010)*.

Policy support

In order to attract privately offered fund companies, multiple locations have implemented preferential policies. Shanghai announced the *Notice on Matters Concerning the Industrial and Commercial Registration of Equity Investment Enterprises in Shanghai* in 2008. Nine policies were adopted to support private securities investment funds, private equity funds, and venture capital funds. It aimed at promoting the establishment of the capital market and transformed Shanghai into an international funding and asset management center. In 2009, Shanghai announced the *Provisions on Concentrating the Financial Resources, Strengthening the Financial Services, and Promoting the Development of the Financial Sector in Shanghai*. Several incentive mechanisms, support measures, and innovation awards were implemented to attract financial talents and institutions. There have been several preferential tax policies. Some financial practitioners receive tax rebates of personal income tax. This policy was adopted to reduce the tax rate to the levels in Hong Kong and Singapore, between 21%–25%.

Shenzhen had once been regarded as the "paradise for privately offered funds" before other locations began implementing preferential policies. Seeing the loss of financial institutions, talents, and capital, Shenzhen announced the *Provisions for the Promotion of the Development of Equity Investment Funds* in July 2010 and the *Notice on Matters Concerning the Further Support for the Development of Equity Investment Funds* in December 2010 to promote the development of privately offered funds. The support policies included preferential tax, award schemes, and housing subsidies. In March 2011, the first privately offered fund industry association in China — Shenzhen Private Equity Association — was founded in Shenzhen. The association acts as the bridge between the industry and the government. It would coordinate sunshine private fund companies and promote the development of the industry.

In recent years, a lot of privately offered funds have chosen to register in the North, especially Tianjin, because of the preferential tax policies. Without a doubt, tax is an important factor when sunshine private funds determine their location of registration. Haixin District, Tianjin, was the first to implement the policy in China that investment income of limited partnership is allocated to the partners first before the partners pay their income tax. This can eliminate the problem of double taxation of the partners. In the past, limited partnership companies also needed to pay corporate business tax.

Internationally, hedge funds are also sensitive to tax. Because of preferential tax and operation convenience, in 2010, around 60% of hedge funds were registered in offshore jurisdictions such as the Cayman Islands, the British Virgin Islands, and Bermuda.[5]

Types of sunshine private fund products

Structured products and unstructured products

Sunshine private fund products can be categorized into structured and unstructured.

Structured products classified investors into different levels, who bear a different degree of risk and receive a different amount of returns. Investors, as priority beneficiaries, receive fixed returns and bear less risk. To them, the product is similar to a fixed return financial product. The fund company, as general beneficiary, receives the majority of the return after allocating returns to investors. This type of product is, in fact, the product offered by the "Shanghai model." Fund companies are required to invest a certain proportion of capital as guarantee funds.

Unstructured products are also called management products. These products operate in the following manner: The fund company needs not provide guarantee funds. It only acts as the investment consultant of securities trust products. It charges an administration fee (usually 1%–1.5%) and receives a proportion of the returns on the trust plan (usually 20% of the excess returns as performance pay). Such trust products do not guarantee returns. The investors bear all the investment risk and receive the majority of the returns. This corresponds to the "Shenzhen model."

As of the end of May 2011, unstructured products of sunshine private funds dominated the market with a share of 77% while structured products only took up 23% (See Fig. 6.12). The domination can be explained by the flexibility of unstructured products .Their size can be more easily expanded thanks to a longer duration. Especially for the open-end funds, purchase and redemption of securities are possible within the duration period. Also, the risk is shared. The fund company needs not bear extra risk.

Fig. 6.12   Percentage share of structured and unstructured products

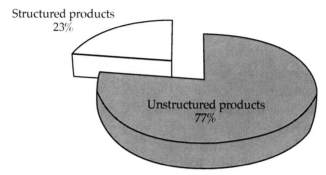

Source: Data from Wind Info analyzed by the Private Fund Research Center of Hua Ming Chuangfu Fund (HMC Fund).

Apart from mainstream structured and unstructured trust products, there are also innovative products being developed in the sunshine private fund market. Trusts of trusts (TOT) and limited partnership fund products have become the focus of development.

As the name suggests, the investment scope of TOT is trust products. TOT has become the synonym of funds which invest in sunshine private fund products. Since the launch of the first TOT in China — Donghai Shengshi No.1 Collective Trust Funds — by China Ping An Trust & Investment Co., Ltd., in May 2009, in two years' time up to May 2011, 53 TOT products have been launched. The rapid development is astounding. The advantages of TOT lie in the diversification of investments, low investment threshold, and multiple regulators. However, at this stage, the development of cross-platform trust is immature and the options available are limited. Investment management is still in the exploratory stage. Moreover, the current TOT aim at risk-control and are more conservative in investments.

Limited partnership sunshine private funds abide by the *Partnership Enterprise Law*. They are sunshine private funds founded by one general partner (fund management company) and not more than 49 limited partners (investors). Investors bear limited liability. The fund management company bears unlimited liability for the operation and debts of the fund. Under this mode of operation, the fund management company is not subject to the laws and legal regulations on trusts.

Limited partnership has long been the prevalent operation mode of foreign hedge funds. In China, limited partnership fund products did not begin to develop until trust companies were suspended from opening new securities accounts in July 2009. In less than two years, more than 30 limited partnership fund products were launched. As limited partnership fund products are not restricted by securities accounts, the future development of the products looks promising.

Types of investment

According to Wind Info, as of May 2011, 99% of the sunshine private fund products in the market were stock sunshine private funds. There were very few bond sunshine private funds (Fig. 6.13). For public funds, stock funds took up 51%. The remaining were bond funds, hybrid funds, money market funds, and other types of funds (See Fig. 6.14).

Fig. 6.13   Percentage share of various types of sunshine private funds

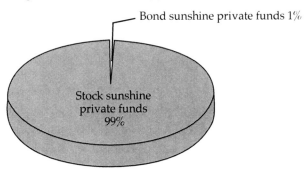

Source: Data from Wind Info analyzed by the Private Fund Research Center of Hua Ming Chuangfu Fund (HMC Fund).

Fig. 6.14   Percentage share of various types of public funds

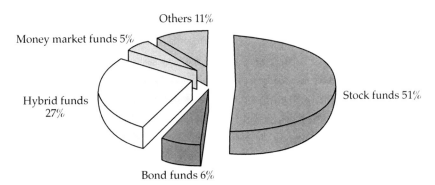

Source: Data from Wind Info analyzed by the Private Fund Research Center of Hua Ming Chuangfu Fund (HMC Fund).

Market concentration of the sunshine private fund management industry

The market concentration of an industry refers to the concentration of industrial production and business. It is usually represented by the proportion of the factors of production or sales of the major enterprise of the industry to those of the whole industry. The industrial organization theory uses industrial concentration as an important indicator of market competition. The logic is as follows: A higher concentration represents higher sales or economic activities are controlled by a small number of enterprises. Those enterprises dominate the market, especially in price determination. Therefore, those enterprises have a certain ability to monopolize the market, and the market is less competitive. The size of assets under management (AUM) and the number of products are two main factors in the analysis of industrial concentration of privately offered funds.

Assets under management

As of the first half of 2011, there are approximately 520 companies which had released securities-type trust products. The AUM of the sunshine private fund industry reached CNY142 billion. Of the 520 companies, 6% held 57% of AUM of the industry. The remaining 94% of companies only held 43% of the AUM of the industry. In terms of AUM, the market concentration of privately offered fund industry is high. Globally, in 2010, the top 1% of hedge fund companies held 70% of the AUM of the industry.

Number of products

As of the end of May 2011, there were 253 privately offered fund companies which had only launched one fund product, accounting for 56.7% of the sunshine private fund companies. There were also a lot of companies which had released more than 20 fund products. The first echelon of sunshine private funds is slowly forming. Table 6.2 shows the top 10 privately offered fund companies by the number of products launched.

The Herfindahl-Hirschman Index (HHI) is an index to measure industrial concentration. It is the sum of the squares of the percentage share of every market participant in the total income and total assets. It measures the change in market shares, which represents the dispersion of companies in the market. The higher the HHI, the higher the degree of concentration and monopoly.

Table 6.2   Top 10 privately offered fund companies by the number of products launched

Rank	Company	Number of products
1	Shanghai Elegant Investment Co., Ltd.	36
2	Rosefinch Investment & Development Center Partnership Ltd.	33
3	Beijing StarRock Investment Management Co., Ltd.	28
4	Springs Capital (Beijing) Ltd.	27
5	Shanghai Congrong Investment Management Co., Ltd.	26
6	Yunnan International Trust Co., Ltd.	25
7	Shenzhen Wudang Asset Management Ltd.	22
8	Bohong (Tianjin) Fund Management Co., Ltd.	20
9	Shanghai Huili Asset Management Co., Ltd.	19
10	Shanghai Vstone Investment Consulting Co., Ltd.	19

Source: Data from Wind Info analyzed by the Private Fund Research Center of Hua Ming Chuangfu Fund (HMC Fund).

Based on the percentage share of fund products in the total products, the HHI of China's sunshine private fund industry is 59.7. The relatively low value is due to the low entry threshold of the industry. A lot of new products are launched by smaller companies. The HHI of public funds is 198.6.

Public fund products are more concentrated than the private fund products. However, the HHIs of both types of products are below 500. According to the U.S. Department of Justice's classification of market structures, both markets are considered competitive (See Table 6.3). This is to say that the competition is keen in terms of the launch of products in the fund industry.

Table 6.3   Classification of market structures based on the Herfindahl-Hirschman Index

Market structure	Oligopoly				Competitive market	
	Highly oligopolistic Type I	Highly oligopolistic Type II	Slightly oligopolistic Type I	Slightly oligopolistic Type II	Competitive Type I	Competitive Type II
HHI value	HHI>3,000	3,000>HHI>1,800	1,800>HHI>1,400	1,400>HHI>1,000	1,000>HHI>500	500>HHI

Source: U.S. Department of Justice, http://www.justice.gov/atr/public/testimony/hhi.htm.

Performance Analysis of the Sunshine Private Fund Industry

This performance analysis is based on public data of sunshine private funds for two reasons: First, of all private securities investment funds, only sunshine private funds have available data. Second, there are increasingly more many private securities investment funds which are sunshine private funds. Sunshine private funds have caught the attention of the public thanks to their impressive performance. We analyze the performance of sunshine private funds and compare it with that of public funds. In the past four years, privately offered funds have experienced a round of CBBC conversion. This allows for a more detailed analysis of privately offered funds. The analysis focuses on three aspects: returns on the products, fluctuation of the returns, and the rate of return under downside risk and risk adjustment.

Analysis of the rate of return on sunshine private funds

Average rate of return on sunshine private funds

In the past four years, the market experienced a round of CBBC conversion. The SSE Composite Index climbed 99.66% in 2007. In 2008, the bearish market drove the SSE Composite Index down by 65.39%. In 2009, in the face of an economic crisis, loose monetary policies injected sufficient fluidity into the A-share market. The SSE Composite Index grew almost 80% that year. In 2010, contractionary monetary policies shocked the A-share market. The SSE Composite Index dropped 14.31% that year. The drop was the third largest in the world, right behind Greece and Spain. The trend of sunshine private funds was similar to that of large-cap shares (See Fig. 6.15).

In 2007 and 2009 when the market rose, the average rates of return on sunshine private funds were 74.16% and 53.81%, respectively. Although the rates of return were lower than the rise in the SSE Composite Index and the CSI 300 Index, the drop in the rate of return on sunshine private funds was 31.7%, smaller than that of the broader markets, in the bearish market in 2008. The ability to control downside risk was evident.

In 2010 when the broader market dropped 14.31%, sunshine private funds attained a positive average rate of return of 5.82%. Sunshine private funds pursue absolute returns. Therefore, downside risk should be under strict control. Its sensitivity to downside risk also reduces its rising power. It is characteristic of sunshine private funds to have smaller rises and slower drops in their rate of return.

Compared to public funds during the same period of time, the performance of sunshine private funds was not lacking. Except for 2007 when the rise in the average rate of return was lower than that of public funds (89.85%), it was on average four percentage points higher than that of public funds during 2008–2010. Looking at individual products, the performance of sunshine private funds was impressive. Apart from 2007 when China Dragon was outperformed by Wang Yawei's Select Huaxia Securities Investment Fund, the best performing sunshine private fund outperformed public funds.

Fig. 6.15   Comparison of the average rates of return on public funds and sunshine private funds, 2007–2010

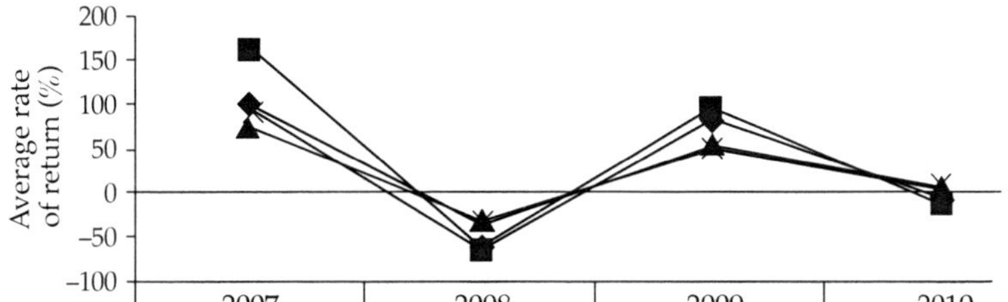

	2007	2008	2009	2010
SSE Composite Index ◆	96.66%	−65.39%	79.98%	−14.31%
CSI 300 Index ■	161.55%	−65.95%	96.71%	−12.51%
Sunshine private funds ▲	74.16%	−31.70%	53.81%	5.82%
Public funds ✕	89.85%	−36.36%	47.40%	3.22%

Source: Data from Wind Info analyzed by the Private Fund Research Center of Hua Ming Chuangfu Fund (HMC Fund).

In summary, in a bull market, the rate of return on public funds is higher than on sunshine private funds. However, in a bear market or in market shock, the performance of sunshine private funds is better. This can be explained by the difference in goals and operation strategy of privately offered funds and public funds. Privately offered funds pursue absolute returns and withdraw when the goals are achieved. Public funds pursue relative returns (relative ranking in the industry is very important for the public fund managers). In a bull market, public funds try to outperform one another, which is why public funds generally have a higher rate of return. In a bear market, privately offered funds can hold bear positions, but public funds are constrained by the positions they can hold and therefore have greater difficulty in controlling loss. In market shock, privately offered funds have flexible operation. They are more capable for grasping structure opportunities.

The fluctuation of the performance of sunshine private funds is less than that of global hedge funds. In recent years, apart from a 15% loss recorded in 2008, the fluctuations have been around 10%.

Performance of sunshine private funds

As of the end of May 2011, the performances of brokerage collection management, sunshine private funds, and public funds are analyzed in periods of six months, one year, two years, and three years. The performance of sunshine private funds is impressive (See Fig. 6.16).

Fig. 6.16   Average annual rate of return on global hedge funds

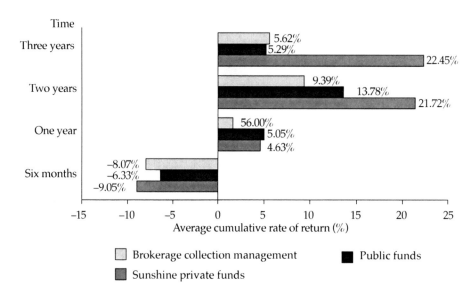

Source: Data from Wind Info analyzed by the Private Fund Research Center of Hua Ming Chuangfu Fund (HMC Fund).

Since 2011, in order to control inflation, the central bank has continued to raise the reserve requirement ratio. Monetary policies have been predominantly contractionary. Influenced by the continuous turmoil in overseas markets, the performance of the A-share market remains sluggish. The performance of sunshine private funds in the last six months was relatively poor with a drop of 9%. Over the same period of time, the drop in public funds was slightly smaller.

Looking at the average rate of return over the past one year, the performances of public funds and sunshine private funds were similar. The advantage of sunshine private funds is more prominent if a longer period of time is considered. As of the end of May 2011, sunshine private funds had attained an average cumulative rate of return of 21.72% over the past two years, higher than that of public funds at 13.78%. In the past three years, the average cumulative rate of return of sunshine private funds (22.45%) is significantly better than that of public funds (5.29%) and brokerage collective management (5.62%).

Distribution of the rates of return on sunshine private funds

As of the end of May 2011, looking at the distribution of the rates of return on sunshine private funds, the performance of the funds had been lackluster in the past six months due to continued market downturn. Most of the products attained a negative rate of return predominantly falling between –15% and 0% (See Fig. 6.17). Only 10% of products attained a positive rate of return. In the most recent six months, the best performing product had a rate of return of 27.33%, and the worst performing had a rate of return of –38.12%, a difference of 65.45 percentage points.

Fig. 6.17   **Distribution of rates of return on sunshine private funds in the past six months as of May 31, 2011**

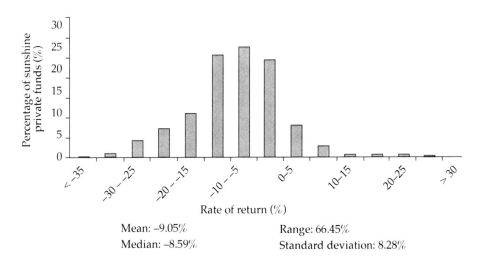

Mean: –9.05%   Range: 66.45%
Median: –8.59%   Standard deviation: 8.28%

Source: Data from Wind Info analyzed by the Private Fund Research Center of Hua Ming Chuangfu Fund (HMC Fund).

If the study period is lengthened to one year, the performance of sunshine private funds is a lot better. As of the end of May 2011, the average rate of return (mean) was 4.63%, and 65% of products attained a positive rate of return. The highest rate of return was 80.12% and the lowest was –36.22%. The difference between the highest and lowest rates of return was 116.34 percentage points. The distribution of rates of return was less concentrated compared to the data when the study period was only six months. The standard deviation expanded to 13.41% (See Fig. 6.18).

Fig. 6.18   Distribution of rates of return on sunshine private funds in the past one year as of May 31, 2011

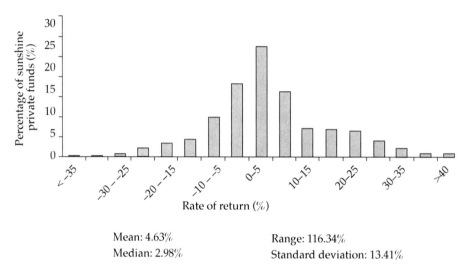

Mean: 4.63%   Range: 116.34%
Median: 2.98%   Standard deviation: 13.41%

Source: Data from Wind Info analyzed by the Private Fund Research Center of Hua Ming Chuangfu Fund (HMC Fund).

In the study period of three years, the features of distribution of the rate of return of sunshine private funds are significantly different from those in a shorter period of study. On one hand, the average rate of return (mean) increased to 22.45%, and almost 75% of products recorded a positive rate of return. On the other hand, the concentration of the distribution of rates of return dropped dramatically. The standard deviation was 32.73%. The range of rates of return was also enlarged with the highest at 113.56%. The difference between the highest and lowest was 160.64 percentage points (See Fig. 6.19).

The polarizing rates of return can be explained by the difference in the quality, size, and investment capabilities of fund management companies. Large fund management companies manage more than RMB2 billion funds. The size is comparable to that of a small public fund company. They usually have a better team. Small privately offered fund companies can be only managing RMB10 million funds. Their investment, research, and risk control capabilities are far below those of the leading companies.

Fig. 6.19   Distribution of rates of return on sunshine private funds in the past three years as of May 31, 2011

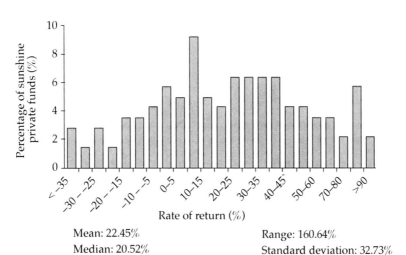

Mean: 22.45%   Range: 160.64%
Median: 20.52%   Standard deviation: 32.73%

Source: Data from Wind Info analyzed by the Private Fund Research Center of Hua Ming Chuangfu Fund (HMC Fund).

Performance comparison of different types of sunshine private funds

The investment strategies and direction of fund products are predominantly determined by the fund manager. Based on the background of the fund manager, sunshine private funds are classified into three types: former public fund managers; former employees of brokerages or fund managers from large securities companies; and private fund managers who were traders or handled discretionary accounts in the early days of China's capital market. They grew with the capital market and have a number of clients. There are also fund managers from banks, trust companies, insurance companies, and financial media.

In terms of proportion, former public fund managers and former employees of brokerages take up a larger share than private fund managers. Former public fund managers prefer portfolio investment and asset allocation. The majority of fund managers in sunshine private fund companies are former public fund managers. Some of the representatives are Jiang Hui of Beijing StarRock Investment Management, Lü Jun of Shanghai Congrong Investment Management, and Shi Bo of Shanghai Elegant Investment. Most of the fund managers are former employees of brokerages, especially broker researchers. Representatives are Luo Weiguang and Zhu Que of Shanghai Elegant Investment. Grassroots private fund managers are more experienced and practical in making investments. They are good at making an analysis of techniques. The turnover rate is high. Representatives include Lin Yuan and Chang Shibin.

Managers with different backgrounds have different investment styles. The rates of return vary to a large extent. As of the end of May 2011, the average rates of return of products managed by managers of different backgrounds over the periods of six months, one year, and three years are shown in Fig. 6.20.

Fig. 6.20   Average rates of return on products managed by managers of different backgrounds over periods of different lengths

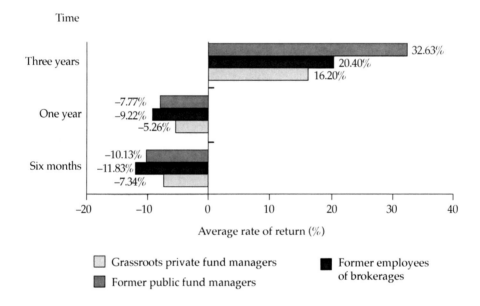

Source: Data from Wind Info analyzed by the Private Fund Research Center of Hua Ming Chuangfu Fund (HMC Fund).

In the short run, the difference in the performances of the various types of sunshine private funds was small, but it becomes more prominent over a longer period of time. The funds managed by grassroots private managers suffer a smaller loss in the short run (six months to one year) but also achieve a small growth in the long run (three years). The funds managed by former employees of brokerages suffer the greatest loss in the short run, the rate of return in the long run is medium. The funds managed by former public fund managers attain a medium rate of return in the short run, but that rate of return in the long run is a lot higher than that of the other two types at 33%.

The average rates of return of the three types of sunshine private funds during 2007–2010 are shown in Fig. 6.21. It can be seen that the performances were similar in the market shock in 2010. The difference was small in 2009. In the bear market in 2008, the funds managed by grassroots managers suffered the greatest loss of –46.38% while those managed by former public fund managers suffered the least loss of –34.80%.

Fig. 6.21   Average rates of return on the three types of sunshine private funds during 2007–2010

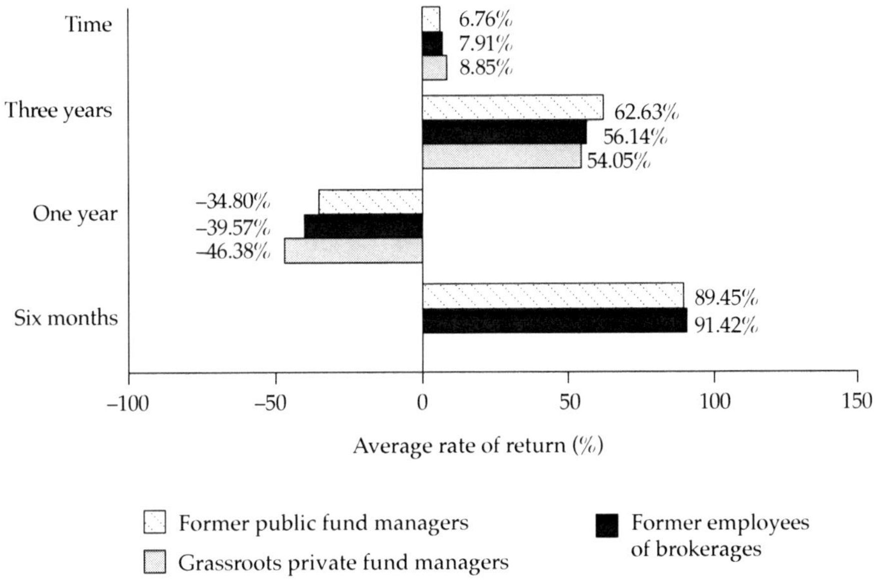

Note: Data for products managed by grassroots managers in 2007 was unavailable.

Source: Data from Wind Info analyzed by the Private Fund Research Center of Hua Ming Chuangfu Fund (HMC Fund).

Comparison of the rates of return on structured and unstructured products of sunshine private funds

As of the end of May 2011, the average rates of return on structured and unstructured products in the most recent six months, one year, and three years have been similar. In the long run (three years), the rate of return on unstructured products is higher than that of structured products (See Fig. 6.22).

Fig. 6.22   Comparison of the average rates of return on structured and unstructured products over periods of different lengths

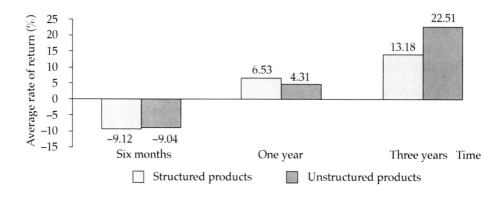

Source: Data from Wind Info analyzed by the Private Fund Research Center of Hua Ming Chuangfu Fund (HMC Fund).

Looking at the data from 2007 to 2010, unstructured products had a smaller drop in the bear market in 2008, but their growth in the rising market was also smaller (See Fig. 6.23). Overall, the performance of structured products was weaker than that of unstructured products.

Fig. 6.23   Comparison of the average rates of return on structured and unstructured products, 2007–2010

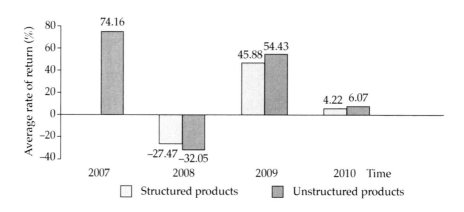

Note: Data for the rate of return on structured products in 2007 was unavailable.
Source: Data from Wind Info analyzed by the Private Fund Research Center of Hua Ming Chuangfu Fund (HMC Fund).

Comparison of the rates of return on sunshine private funds launched in different years

As of the end of May 2011, the difference in the annualized rate of return on sunshine private funds launched in different years was great (See Table 6.4). The annualized rate of return on products launched in 2007 or before was high and that on products launched in 2009 and after was low. Table 6.5 shows the comparison with public funds over the same period of time. The mean and the highest rate of return of sunshine private funds have been higher than those of public funds. However, the percentage of funds which obtained a positive rate of return was lower. This implies that the difference in the quality of sunshine private funds was larger.

Public funds were developed earlier. So older public funds were launched more than 10 years ago and have experienced two market cycles. The average annualized rate of return on those public funds was 17.75%. The highest annualized rate of return was 22.12%. There was no substantial difference from the mean. Horizontal differentiation was small.

The annualized rate of return on foreign hedge funds during 1993–2010 was 9%. Over the same period of time, that of the U.S. mutual funds was 4.36%.

Table 6.4 **Annualized rate of return on sunshine private funds launched at different times as of May 2011 (%)**

Date of establishment	Annualized rate of return			Percentage of funds with a positive rate of return (%)
	Mean	Median	Highest rate of return	
Before 2007	23.36	25.75	38.54	100
2007	7.63	7.27	27.84	77
2008	14.45	11.62	65.30	85
2009	9.28	7.22	57.97	82
2010	0.67	–0.72	—	46
Jan–May 2011	–10.55	–5.75	—	12

Note: The majority of funds launched in 2010 and the first five months of 2011 have been in the market for less than a year. Therefore, their annualized rate of return is not suitable for statistical comparisons.

Source: Data from Wind Info analyzed by the Private Fund Research Center of Hua Ming Chuangfu Fund (HMC Fund).

Table 6.5   Annualized rate of return on public funds launched at different times as of May 2011 (%)

Date of establishment	Annualized rate of return			Percentage of funds with a positive rate of return
	Mean	Median	Highest rate of return	
2001	17.75	17.78	22.12	100
2002	19.43	20.83	24.36	100
2003	17.89	19.11	30.97	100
2004	21.17	23.51	55.85	100
2005	20.15	24.69	44.92	100
2006	18.25	20.29	41.20	99
2007	4.17	3.39	16.91	79
2008	12.73	9.23	46.92	99
2009	2.97	3.90	28.18	72
2010	−2.65	0.36	—	53
Jan–May 2011	−7.24	0.00	—	32

Note: The majority of funds launched in 2010 and the first five months of 2011 have been in the market for less than a year. Therefore, their annualized rate of return is not suitable for statistical comparisons.

Source: Data from Wind Info analyzed by the Private Fund Research Center of Hua Ming Chuangfu Fund (HMC Fund).

Fluctuation in the ranking of performance

Although the overall performance of sunshine private funds in the long or short run, or in the bear or bull market has been average, further studies of a single product revealed the following: A product that does well in the short run cannot keep up its performance in the long run, and vice versa; a product that does well in the bull market does not perform well in the bear market, and vice versa. The fluctuation of the ranking of the products' performance is great and performance is difficult to maintain.

As shown in Table 6.6 and Table 6.7, only Shitong 1 appeared twice in the top 10 lists. It was ranked third in terms of the annual rate of return as of May 2011 and fourth in terms of the average rate of return in the past three years. It should be noted that some products had not been in the market for more than three years. Therefore, there was no available data. As sunshine private finds have not been developed for a long time, more time is needed to gather sufficient data to evaluate their rate of return.

Table 6.6 Top 10 sunshine private funds by the rate of return in the most recent six months, one year, and three years as of the end of May 2011

Rank	Six months		One year		Three years	
	Product	Rate of return (%)	Product	Rate of return (%)	Product	Rate of return (%)
1	Chengrui 1	27.33	Dinghui 1	80.12	Shangya 4	113.56
2	Bohong 1	24.18	Hongchuang	77.13	Shangya 3	102.07
3	Moerxiang 1	22.98	Shitong 1	64.99	Longteng	98.83
4	Hongchuang	16.96	Deyuanan Strategic Growth 1	62.75	Shitong 1	89.24
5	Xinhe East	16.08	Zexi Ruijin 1	44.97	New Value 2 (Guangdong Finance)	88.70
6	Bao'an 1	14.73	Changjin 3	40.05	New Value 3	87.95
7	Jingliang Energy China Lanhai 3	13.15	Chaos 2	38.92	Zhuque 2 (SZITIC)	86.75
8	Shenqian 1	11.83	Linyuan	38.59	Springs Capital 2008	85.85
9	Huafu Liqin 1	11.20	Zhanbo 1	36.29	Zhuque 1 (SZITIC)	84.48
10	Bangsheng 1	10.11	Tajin Tiger 1	35.63	Shangya 1 (SZITIC)	83.52

Source: Data from Wind Info analyzed by the Private Fund Research Center of Hua Ming Chuangfu Fund (HMC Fund).

Table 6.7 Top 10 sunshine private funds by the rate of return, 2007–2010

Rank	2007		2008	
	Product	Rate of return (%)	Product	Rate of return (%)
1	China Dragon	216.44	Jinzhonghe Xiding	23.97
2	China Dragon Stable	166.11	Jujin 2	13.89
3	China Dragon Aggressive	138.54	StarRock 3	4.29
4	Huili Jiaji 1	102.79	StarRock 2	4.18
5	China Opportunities 1 (Ping An)	98.89	StarRock 1	4.02
6	Greewoods Stable	95.43	Xianjin Fengli	3.47
7	Yilong China 1	78.01	China Dragon Select	3.12

Table 6.7   Top 10 sunshine private funds by the rate of return, 2007–2010

(Cont'd)

Rank	2007		2008	
	Product	Rate of return (%)	Product	Rate of return (%)
9	Mingda Capital Management	71.99	Strategic Growth 2007 3	0.20
10	Lighthorse	69.33	Index Strengthening 2007 1	0.00

Rank	2009		2010	
	Product	Rate of return (%)	Product	Rate of return (%)
1	New Value 2 (Guangdong Finance)	192.57	Shitong 1	86.16
2	New Value 1	156.47	Pujiang Star 6	75.52
3	Shangya 4	140.08	Dinghui 1	69.10
4	Chaos 1 (ZRITC)	139.53	Huabao 1	47.80
5	Longwin Hongli 2	135.24	Chaos 2	47.21
6	Shangya 2	132.88	Licheng Fengjing 2	44.71
7	Kaibao 1	121.21	Deyuanan Strategic Growth 1	42.92
8	Springs Capital Growth 1	121.03	Ruitian Value Growth	39.95
9	New Value 3	120.89	Heju 1	39.51
10	Longteng	120.35	Zhanbo 1	38.77

Source: Data from Wind Info analyzed by the Private Fund Research Center of Hua Ming Chuangfu Fund (HMC Fund).

Rate of fluctuation of return on sunshine private funds and downside risk

Rate of fluctuation of return

The rate of fluctuation of return is an important indicator to measure the risk of fund products. It is also the most commonly used risk evaluation indicator. The difference in the distribution of the rate of fluctuation of return on sunshine private funds and public funds in the past one year as of the end of May 2011 was large. About 99% of public fund products had a rate of fluctuation of return between 0 and 0.04. In comparison, the distribution of that of sunshine private funds was much greater (See Fig. 6.24).

Fig. 6.24   Distribution of the rates of fluctuation of return on sunshine private funds and public funds in the past one year as of the end of May 2011

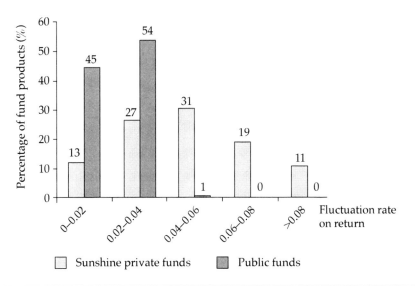

	Sunshine private funds	Public funds
Mean	0.049	0.018
Highest rate of fluctuation	0.210	0.058

Source: Data from Wind Info analyzed by the Private Fund Research Center of Hua Ming Chuangfu Fund (HMC Fund).

The mean and median of the rate of fluctuation of return on sunshine private funds were larger than on public funds. This corresponds to the investment styles of the two types of funds. Overall, public funds are more conservation and sunshine private funds are more willing to take risk in order to obtain a greater return.

As the size and risk differ among products to a large extent, comparison is made by classifying sunshine private funds and public funds into different types. The top 10 sunshine private fund companies by the number of products, together with Shanghai Chongyang Investment Management and Zexi Investment, are considered the first echelon. Those which have issued 10 to 20 products are considered the second echelon. Companies in the first echelon have assets of over RMB2 billion. The products are compared with the medium equity products of public funds which hold RMB2 billion to RMB5 billion in assets (See Fig. 6.25 and Fig. 6.26). The products of second echelon are compared with the small equity products of public funds which hold RMB1 billion to RMB2 billion assets (See Fig. 6.27 and Fig. 6.28). The data are for the past one year as of the end of May 2011.

Fig. 6.25   Risk-return distribution of the sunshine private fund products of the first echelon

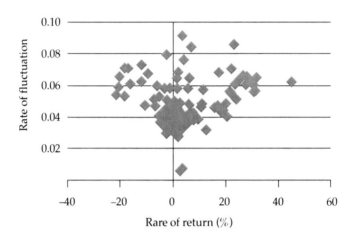

Source: Data from Wind Info analyzed by the Private Fund Research Center of Hua Ming Chuangfu Fund (HMC Fund).

Fig. 6.26   Risk-return distribution of the products of the public funds which held RMB2 billion to RMB5 billion

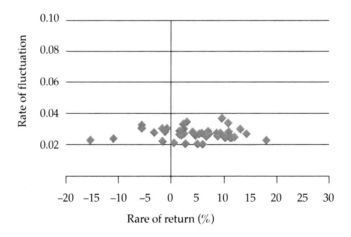

Source: Data from Wind Info analyzed by the Private Fund Research Center of Hua Ming Chuangfu Fund (HMC Fund).

Fig. 6.27   Risk-return distribution of the sunshine private fund products of the second echelon

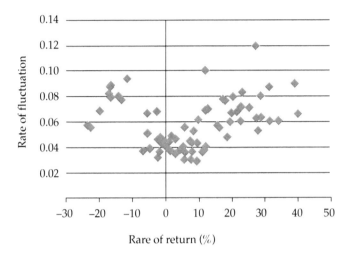

Source: Data from Wind Info analyzed by the Private Fund Research Center of Hua Ming Chuangfu Fund (HMC Fund).

Fig. 6.28   Risk-return distribution of the products of the public funds which held RMB1 billion to RMB2 billion

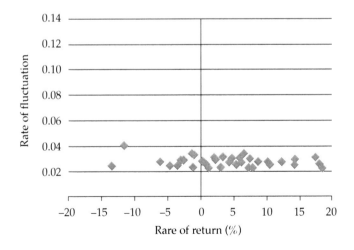

Source: Data from Wind Info analyzed by the Private Fund Research Center of Hua Ming Chuangfu Fund (HMC Fund).

From the graphs, the distribution of rate of return on both types of funds is scattered. The average rate of return on the sunshine private fund products of first echelon and medium equity product of public funds were approximately 5.4%. The average rate of fluctuation of the latter was 2.8%, slightly lower than that of the former at 4.4%.

Comparing the risk-return distribution of sunshine private fund products in the second echelon and small equity products of public funds (See Fig. 6.27 and Fig. 6.28), it can be seen that the rate of fluctuation of small public funds was more concentrated at a lower level than that of the sunshine private fund products. The average rate of fluctuation of the former was 0.028 and that of the latter was 0.057. While sunshine private fund products bear higher risk, they obtained a greater return. The average rate of return stood at 6.64%, higher than that of the small public fund products and the sunshine private fund products in the first echelon.

Using the rate of fluctuation to represent risk, its relationship with the rate of return on sunshine private funds during 2007–2010 is shown in Fig. 6.29, Fig. 6.30, Fig. 6.31, and Fig. 6.32.

Fig. 6.29   Risk-return relationship of sunshine private funds, 2007

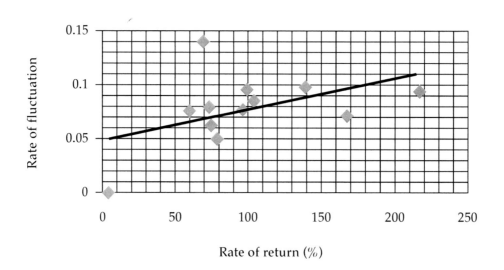

Source: Data from Wind Info analyzed by the Private Fund Research Center of Hua Ming
        Chuangfu Fund (HMC Fund).

Fig. 6.30   Risk-return relationship of sunshine private funds, 2008

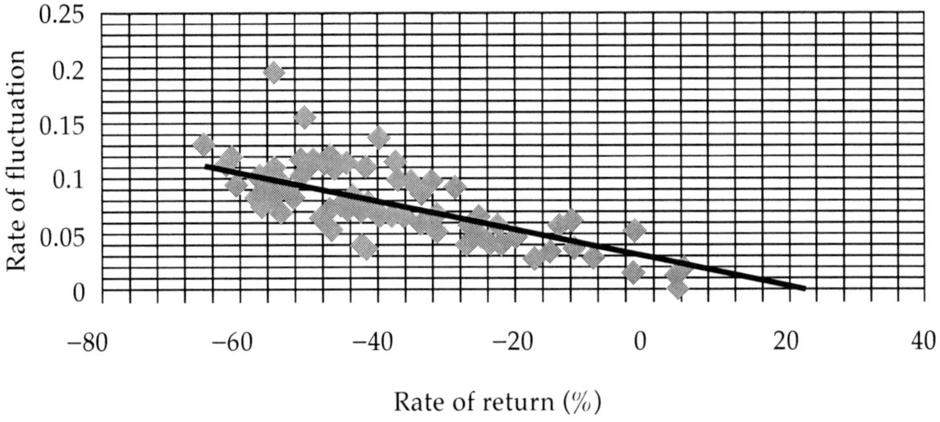

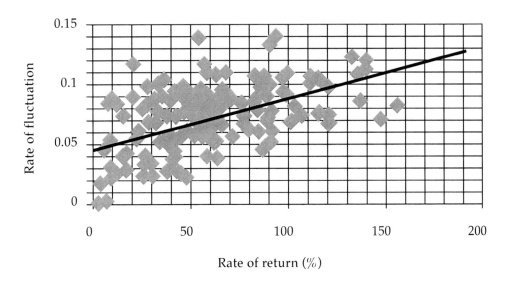

Source: Data from Wind Info analyzed by the Private Fund Research Center of Hua Ming
Chuangfu Fund (HMC Fund).

Fig. 6.31   Risk-return relationship of sunshine private funds, 2009

Source: Data from Wind Info analyzed by the Private Fund Research Center of Hua Ming
Chuangfu Fund (HMC Fund).

Fig. 6.32   Risk-return relationship of sunshine private funds, 2010

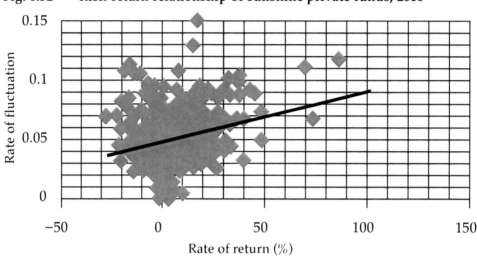

Source: Data from Wind Info analyzed by the Private Fund Research Center of Hua Ming
        Chuangfu Fund (HMC Fund).

In 2007, 2009, and 2010, the risk and return were in direct proportion. This complied with the high-risk, high-return principle. In 2008, the risk and return were in indirect proportion. Products with higher risk had a lower rate of return. The violation of the principle was not difficult to explain. The high-risk, high return principle refers to the expected risk and expected return. In 2008, all the markets were in a downturn. Such systemic risk could hardly be foreseen by investors.

The products which bore high risk to obtain a high return in 2007 continued to adopt the same strategy in 2008. Their aggressive investment strategy was what caused their downfall. More conservative products bearing a lower risk were more concerned about risk control. Their rate of return suffered a smaller drop in 2008. This is why sunshine private funds had a negative risk-return relationship in 2008.

A number of sunshine private funds products have the features of low risk, high return. Risk is well controlled and a high growth rate is maintained. This can bring about excess return per unit of risk. This is an important factor in product rating.

Downside risk

Sunshine private funds pursue absolute return, which requires a strict control over downside risk. Downside risk represents the potential decline for the net value of the fund to decline, or the loss that could be sustained as a result of such potential decline. Upward fluctuation is not counted. This aligns risk in mathematical calculations and risk encountered by investors. The formula for calculating downside risk of the funds here is adopted from Wind Info.

$$DR_i = \sqrt{(1/(n-1))\sum_{t=1}^{n} (\min\{R_{it} - R_f, 0\})^2}$$

Of which n is the number of samples, R_{it} is the rate of return at the time t. R_f is the rate of return without risk.

The smaller the value, the lower the downside risk.

The industry is paying more attention to this risk measurement indicator. The evaluation of a fund product (e.g., selection process of the Golden Bull Fund Award) takes into account the product's ability to yield long-term return and control downside risk. Compared to public funds, privately offered funds are more flexible with positions and better at controlling downside risk. They are able to restrict the loss when the market is falling.

As of the end of May 2011, the distribution of downside risk of sunshine private funds and public funds in the past year is shown in Fig. 6.33. It reveals that distribution of downside risk of public funds concentrated in the two ends of the continuum. In other words, most products bore low or high risk, and few bore moderate risk. More than 40% of the products had downside risk falling in the range of 0.4–0.5. It is the opposite for sunshine private funds. The distribution of downside risk concentrated in the moderate range. Noticeably, 37% of products had downside risk in the range of 0.2–0.3. Despite the difference in distribution, the values of downside risk of sunshine private funds and public funds were close at around 0.3. There were 18 sunshine private funds which had 0 downside risk, which was difficult to achieve in a market with short selling or hedging mechanisms.

The distribution of downside risk of sunshine private fund products in the first echelon and medium equity products of public funds are shown in Fig. 6.34 and Fig. 6.35, while that of sunshine private fund products in the second echelon and small equity products of public funds are shown in Fig. 6.36 and Fig. 6.37.

Fig. 6.33   Distribution of downside risk of sunshine private funds and public funds in the past year as of the end of May 2011

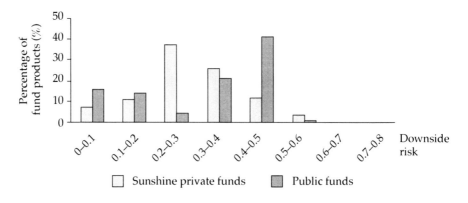

	Sunshine private funds	Public funds
Mean	0.29	0.30
Median	0.27	0.39
Highest value	0.76	0.62

Source: Data from Wind Info analyzed by the Private Fund Research Center of Hua Ming Chuangfu Fund (HMC Fund).

Fig. 6.34   Distribution of downside risk of sunshine private fund products in the first echelon

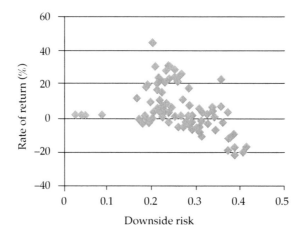

Source: Data from Wind Info analyzed by the Private Fund Research Center of Hua Ming Chuangfu Fund (HMC Fund).

Fig. 6.35   Distribution of downside risk of medium equity products of public funds

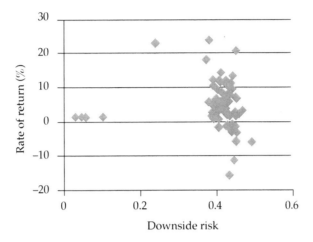

Source: Data from Wind Info analyzed by the Private Fund Research Center of Hua Ming Chuangfu Fund (HMC Fund).

Fig. 6.36   Distribution of downside risk of sunshine private fund products in the second echelon

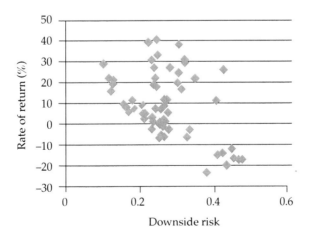

Source: Data from Wind Info analyzed by the Private Fund Research Center of Hua Ming Chuangfu Fund (HMC Fund).

Fig. 6.37 **Distribution of downside risk of small equity products of public funds**

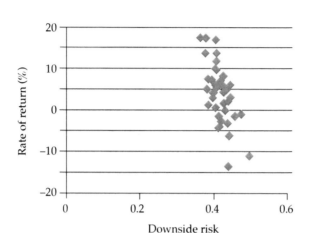

Source: Data from Wind Info analyzed by the Private Fund Research Center of Hua Ming Chuangfu Fund (HMC Fund).

It can be seen from Fig. 6.34 and Fig. 6.35 that the distribution of downside risk of sunshine private fund products of the first echelon was more scattered. The downside risk of medium equity product of public funds concentrated around 0.4 with a mean of 0.42. The downside risk of sunshine private fund products of the first echelon was significantly lower than that of medium equity products of public funds. The former had better downside risk control ability. The distribution of downside risk of sunshine private fund products of the second echelon and small equity product of public funds was similar to their counterparts.

From the temporal perspective, as shown in Fig. 6.38, the difference between the distribution of downside risk of sunshine private funds and public funds was significant during 2007–2010. Whether in a bull market, a bear market, or in market shock, the downside risk of sunshine private funds is smaller than that of public funds. The risk control ability of the former is better.

Risk-adjusted return

To rate a fund product, one cannot look at the rate of return alone. Different rating systems of sunshine private funds do not give top rating to a fund only because of a high return as high net value growth can be achieved under high risk. The higher the expected return, the higher the risk investors have to bear,

Fig. 6.38   Comparison of downside risk of sunshine private funds and public funds, 2007–2010

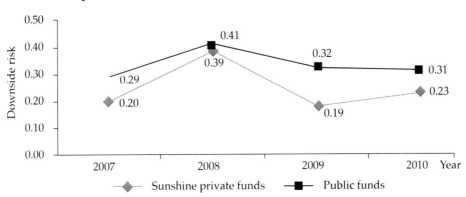

Source: Data from Wind Info analyzed by the Private Fund Research Center of Hua Ming Chuangfu Fund (HMC Fund).

and vice versa. Investors attempt to maximize return under considerable risk or minimize risk with a considerable return. This is reflected by the risk-adjusted return. It takes into account risk and return and eliminates risk factors which have adverse effects on the evaluation of performance.

There are three classic indicators of risk-adjusted return: Sharpe ratio, Treynor ratio, and Jensen ratio.[6] In this study, the Sharpe ratio is chosen to analyze sunshine private funds for three reasons: First, the Sharpe ratio is the most commonly used ratio. Second, the Jensen ratio is based on the same principle as the Sharpe ratio. Third, the Treynor ratio only considers the systemic risk in the product. It is not suitable for sunshine private funds, which do not make fully decentralized investment.

The other risk-adjusted ratio used in this study is the Sortino ratio. At present, the Sortino ratio is more prevalent and has become an important indicator in fund product rating. The fund industry is paying increasingly more attention to downside risk. Downside risk is better at reflecting the concerns investors have for risk.

Sharpe ratio

The Sharpe ratio is based on the capital asset pricing model (CAPM). It was first proposed by William Forsyth Sharpe, the winner of the 1990 Nobel Memorial Prize in Economic Sciences.[7] The core idea is that rational investors would choose and hold effective portfolios to maximize return under a given level of risk, or to minimize risk given a certain return.

The Sharpe ratio is defined as:

$$[E(R_P) - R_f]/\sigma_P$$

Of which $E(R_p)$ is the expected rate of return of the portfolio, R_f is the rate of return without risk, and is the σ_p standard deviation.

The Sharpe ratio represents the excess return of the portfolio per unit of total risk. The higher the Sharpe ratio, the greater the excess return.

As of the end of May 2011, in the past one year, 35% of the sunshine private funds had a Sharpe ratio between –0.5–0. The average of all the funds was –0.29, lower than that of public funds at –0.12. Looking at the past two years, the performance of sunshine private funds was better. The Sharpe ratio of 70% of the funds fell in the range of 0 to 1. The average value of all funds was 0.23. If the period is lengthened to three years, the number of funds with a positive Sharpe ratio and that with a negative Sharpe ratio was similar. The average value was 0.08 (See Fig. 6.39).

Fig. 6.39   **Distribution of the Sharpe ratio of sunshine private funds as of the end of May 2011**

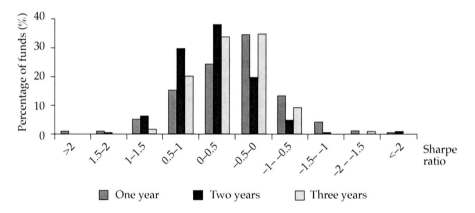

Source: Data from Wind Info analyzed by the Private Fund Research Center of Hua Ming Chuangfu Fund (HMC Fund).

Compared to the distribution of return, the distribution of the Sharpe ratio of sunshine private funds was more concentrated. The difference in the Sharpe ratio was not as great as in the rate of return. Therefore, the Sharpe ratio is more suitable for comparison.

Table 6.8 shows the ranking of sunshine private fund products by their risk-return performance. Those with better performances also perform better in various rating classes in general.

Table 6.8   **Top 10 sunshine private fund products by the Sharpe ratio over different periods of time as of the end of May 2011**

Rank	One year		Two years		Three years	
	Product	Sharpe ratio	Product	Sharpe ratio	Product	Sharpe ratio
1	Pujiang Star 22	2.96	Yifu Growth 1	1.60	StarRock 4	1.05
2	Hongchuang	2.73	Pujiang Star 6	1.49	StarRock 3	1.03
3	Linyuan	2.17	Jingxi 1	1.49	StarRock 5	0.99
4	Dinghui 1	2.06	Chongyang 1	1.37	StarRock 1	0.98
5	Deyuanan Strategic Growth 1	2.02	Xinlanrui	1.36	StarRock 2	0.97
6	Zexi Ruijin	1.94	Chongyang 2	1.34	China Dragon Select	0.86
7	Hongtai Select 1	1.66	Lecheng Select	1.31	Springs Capital 2008	0.81
8	Jinigu Select 1	1.55	Linyuan	1.21	Boyi Select	0.78
9	Jinying 1	1.49	Ruitian Value Growth	1.12	New Value 3	0.73
10	Renhe Huijin 1	1.48	Liuhe Guanghuisuiyue 1	1.10	Greenwoods Stable	0.69

Source: Data from Wind Info analyzed by the Private Fund Research Center of Hua Ming Chuangfu Fund (HMC Fund).

From Table 6.6 and Table 6.8, it can be seen that only half of the products which ranked top 10 considering the rate of return over a period of one year appeared in the top 10 when it comes to the Sharpe ratio. Over the period of three years, only two of the top 10 products in terms of the rate of return could make it to the top 10 in terms of the Sharpe ratio.

Sortino ratio

The only difference between the Sortino ratio and the Sharpe ratio is that the former only considers the downside risk of the fund. In other words, it calculates the excess return on the portfolio per unit of downside risk.[8] The higher the value, the higher the excess return.

The Sortino ratio is calculated as follows:

$$[E(R_P) - R_f]/DR$$

Of which, $E(R_p)$ is the expected rate of return. R_f is the rate of return without risk.

DR is the downside risk.

The distribution of the Sortino ratio of sunshine private funds is shown in Fig. 6.40.

Fig. 6.40   Distribution of the Sortino ratio of sunshine private funds as of the end of May 2011

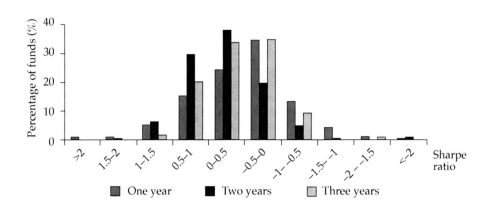

	One year	Two years	Three years
Mean	0.20	0.21	0.19

Source: Data from Wind Info analyzed by the Private Fund Research Center of Hua Ming Chuangfu Fund (HMC Fund).

I can be seen from Fig. 6.40 that the distribution of the Sortino ratio concentrated as the time span lengthens. The Sortino ratio of around 70% of funds concentrated in the range of 0–0.5 over the time periods of two and three years. The average value over three different time periods remained close to 0.2. The average value over a time period of three years was 0.19, a lot higher than that of public funds at 0.02.

Table 6.9 shows the ranking of fund products by the Sortino ratio. The similarity with the ranking by the Sharpe ratio is high. This shows that the two risk measurement ratios are related, to a certain degree.

Table 6.9 Top 10 sunshine private fund products by the Sortino ratio over different periods of time as of the end of May 2011

Rank	One year		Two years		Three years	
	Product	Sortino ratio	Product	Sortino ratio	Product	Sortino ratio
1	Pujiang Star 22	25.64	Sapphire E-4501	3.32	Century Fund 1	0.91
2	Zhanbo1	3.66	Xinlanrui	1.92	StarRock 4	0.73
3	Sapphire E-4501	3.32	Zhongrui Jixiang Guanjia 1	1.33	StarRock 3	0.72
4	Xinyuan Lanzhong	3.27	Yifu Growth	1.14	StarRock 5	0.68
5	Renhe Huijin 1	2.67	Jingxi 1	1.05	StarRock 1	0.67
6	Hongtai Select 1	2.53	Chongyang 1	0.90	StarRock 2	0.67
7	Huifu 35	2.49	Chongyang 2	0.86	New Value 3	0.62
8	Minsen H	2.38	Dinghui 1	0.73	Zhuque 1 (SZITIC)	0.61
9	Hongchuang	2.11	Licheng Fengjing 2	0.69	Shangya 1 (SZITIC)	0.60
10	Dinghui 1	2.01	Qianzhujin chaos 2	0.69	Greenwoods Stable	0.53

Source: Data from Wind Info analyzed by the Private Fund Research Center of Hua Ming Chuangfu Fund (HMC Fund).

Development Direction of the Private Securities Investment Fund Industry

As the private securities investment fund industry develops, market competition becomes more acute. Sunshine private funds are becoming the prevalent type of private securities investment funds, differentiation and innovation take place, sales are getting more attention, and the investment philosophy has changed.

Prevalence of sunshine private funds

Sunshine private funds first emerged in 2004. In February, China Resource SZITIC Trust Co., Ltd., launched the first sunshine private fund — SZITIC Pure Heart China Investment Trust. In a sunshine private fund, the trust company acts as the issuer, the bank as the custodian, and the privately offered fund company raises funds. With new requirements from adaption policies, this new operation mode allows privately offered fund companies to participate in fund management as "investment consultants." Privately offered funds were no longer "underground." Sunshine private funds had evolved to become part of the mainstream of privately offered funds.

Sunshine private funds have been given legal status. Their operation is regulated by law. The regulations require the funds to disclose information and improve their credibility. This makes the funds a major force in China's capital market. At present, as sunshine private funds are in the form of trusts, they are regulated by the laws and regulations of trusts. As the revised *Law on Securities Investment Fund* has been announced, sunshine private funds are likely to be incorporated into the fund regulatory system and gain official approval. This is what private securities investment fund companies hope to see. According to Simuwang, almost 60% of privately offered fund companies considered the lack of legal status the primary obstacle in the development of privately offered funds.

First, sunshine private funds are favorable for the strengthening of the industry. In the short run, privately offered funds which are not sunshine private funds can operate at a low cost and high efficiency. However, as the market and relevant systems mature, increasingly more investors pursue long-term investment. They are more concerned about financial security. Without legal protection, investors are unsure about entrusting privately offered funds with a large amount of money. Such privately offered funds cannot raise a large amount of funds to strengthen themselves.

The information disclosure of sunshine private funds is more comprehensive. This is an advantage for investors as well as a way to raise the quality of investments made by the private securities investment fund industry. This can form a virtuous circle to attract capital.

Second, sunshine private funds help promote the development of the financial market and the fund industry. Privately offered funds which are not sunshine private funds are not required to disclose information. The regulatory system is weak. Market manipulators may attempt to control the market and make malicious speculation. This causes fluctuation of asset prices and disorder in the financial market. Sunshine private funds are more regulated. They are operated in a manner different from public funds. This increases the layers of the market. Sunshine private funds are advantageous for the stability of the financial market.

Sunshine private funds are favorable for the development of the fund industry. Their degree of marketization is higher and would reinforce the competitiveness of the fund market. This would pressure the public funds to improve their service and management quality. In recent years, privately offered funds have attracted a large group of former public fund managers. This has prompted public funds to improve. As a result, the efficiency of the whole fund market improves.

In summary, sunshine private funds are a pathway to the healthy development of the private securities investment funds. They are the direction of future development of the industry.

Differentiated development

Fund companies improve their comparative advantage by offering differentiated products. The uniqueness of products and the reputation of the company (market recognition of the fund managers and outstanding business performance) are the core competitiveness of sunshine private funds. After several years of development, some sunshine private fund companies have exercised their comparative advantage and gained market recognition.

Some sunshine private funds specialize in industry funds of a certain industry. For example, Shanghai Congrong Investment Management Co., Ltd., has launched six unstructured medical sunshine private funds. The funds invest in sub-sectors of health care products, such as medical products, health services, and pharmaceuticals. There are 150 stocks for selection. The investment scope is small compared to the thousands of stocks listed on the Shanghai Stock Exchange and Shenzhen Stock Exchange. Industry funds are more risky than funds which invest in stocks across industries. Such high-risk, high-return sunshine private funds are suitable for investors with considerable risk-bearing ability. These are better allocation funds. Industry funds can help prevent the homogenization of sunshine private funds and repetition of products by the same company. Table 6.10 shows the industry funds of sunshine private funds which had better performances as of June 2011.

Table 6.10   Unstructured industry funds of sunshine private funds which had better performances as of June 2011

Fund	Company	Manager	Date of establishment	Industry
Huabao·Congrong Medical	Shanghai Congrong Investment Management Co., Ltd.	Jiang Guangce	June 30, 2010	Medical and healthcare
Beijing International Trust·Congrong Medical 2	Shanghai Congrong Investment Management Co., Ltd.	Lü Jun	October 11, 2010	Medical and healthcare
China Industrial International Trust·Congrong Medical 5	Shanghai Congrong Investment Management Co., Ltd.	Lü Jun	January 25, 2011	Medical and healthcare
China Resources Szitic Trust·Congrong Medical 3	Shanghai Congrong Investment Management Co., Ltd.	Lü Jun	February 11, 2011	Medical and healthcare
China Foreign Economy and Trade Trust·Congrong Medical Select	Shanghai Congrong Investment Management Co., Ltd.	Lü Jun	March 15, 2011	Medical and healthcare
China Foreign Economy and Trade Trust·Congrong Domestic Medical	Shanghai Congrong Investment Management Co., Ltd.	Jiang Guangce	June 10, 2011	Medical and healthcare
Zhongrong International Trust·Leading Medicine	Leading Fund	Zhu Aiguo	September 28, 2010	Medical and healthcare
China Foreign Economy and Trade Trust·Eastern Consumption Growth	China Foreign Economy and Trade Trust, Co., Ltd.	—	February 22, 2008	Medical and healthcare
China Industrial International Trust·Rosefinch18	Rosefinch Investment	Li Hualun	September 28, 2010	Medical and healthcare
China Industrial International Trust·Rosefinch 17 (TMR Industry Select)	Rosefinch Investment	Zhang Haidi, Shi Hong	October 8, 2010	Technology, media, and telecommunications

Source: Simuwang, http://www.simuwang.com.

There are also privately offered funds which specialize in investing in privately placed products. Privately offered trusts mainly invest in privately offered products of listed companies. Private placement is a financing channel of listed companies. New shares are only offered to selected investors. As the number of selected investors is 10 or below, the requirement for the financial power of investors is high. Usually, only institutions or individuals with strong financial strength can take part in private placement. However, through trust products, the investment threshold can be lowered to RMB1 million. As making investments is becoming more difficult in the secondary market, the emergence of privately offered products targeting the primary market perform very well. In the first half of 2011, while most of the sunshine private fund products were experiencing a downturn, the two products of Bohong Fund Management Co., Ltd., which concentrated on investing in privately offered products performed well. Bohong Private Placement Index Fund 4 obtained the highest rate of return at 36.91%. From the beginning of 2010 to the beginning of 2011, 24 limited partnership companies participated in 40 private placements of 33 companies. The subscription for additional shares amounted to RMB5.25 billion. At present, the companies which are more active in investing in private placements are Bohong Fund Management Co., Ltd., Jiangsu Ruihua Investment Holding Group Company Ltd., and Shanghai Vstone Investment Consulting Co., Ltd. They invest in private placements in the form of limited partnerships.

Differentiation is not only manifested in the types of products but also the investment strategies of the fund. Investment strategies differ among fund companies. Fund products of the same company are managed by different fund managers, who have different investment strategies or styles. Fund managers which have a consistent investment style usually attract investors. The fund managers' capital source is more stable, which is favorable for the long-term fund operation and growth. Some large privately offered fund companies such as Shanghai Elegant Investment Co., Ltd., Shanghai Chongyang Investment Management Co., Ltd., Greenwoods Investment, Rosefinch Investment Co., Ltd., and New Value Investment have established a consistent investment style after several years of development.

Increasing concern about sales

Public funds entered into the realm of privately offered funds through segregated account management in an attempt to gain a share of the high-end financial services. From June 2009 to the end of 2010, 276 one-to-many segregated account management products were launched, which amounted to RMB60 billion.

Brokerage collection management is in a phase of rapid development after the exploration stage. The quantity and product size are continuously expanding (See Fig. 6.41). The fast development of alternative products poses pressure on sunshine private funds.

Fig. 6.41   Development of brokerage collection management products

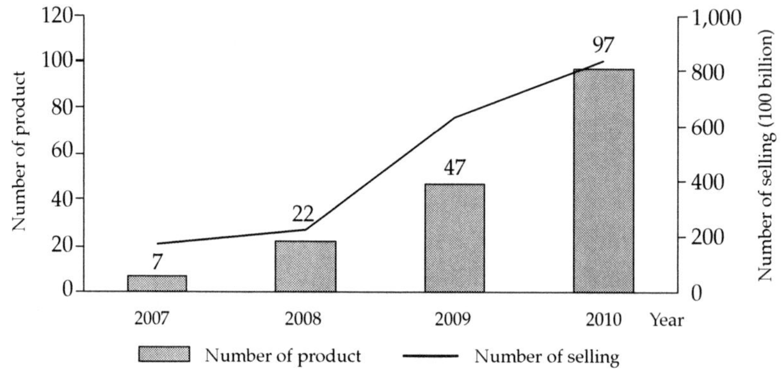

Source: Data from Wind Info analyzed by the Private Fund Research Center of Hua Ming Chuangfu Fund (HMC Fund).

In the face of fierce competition in the industry, the competition behavior of sunshine private funds has changed since its initial development stage. In the initial development stage, privately offered funds attract investors by business performance and the reputation of the fund managers. A lot of privately offered fund companies did not set up a sales department. Investment research staff had to take care of functions such as roadshows and seminars. However, as the industry quickly expanded and competition became fiercer, selling by reputation could not catch up with the development of the companies. The companies began to set up sales teams to explore sales channels and the research staffs were no longer responsible for handling sales. The sales method of sunshine private funds is a combination of direct sales, though brokers, banks, and third-party financial institutions. Private commercial banks and third-party financial institutions are rising stars in the industry. Their potential cannot be underestimated.

Direct sales channels

Direst sales was the earliest sales mode of privately offered funds. Investors directly purchase fund products without intermediaries or agents. The fund companies need not share the subscription fees with intermediaries or agents. It is the sales mode with the lowest cost, and investors have a closer relationship with the fund managers. However, without publicity, sunshine private funds cannot attract a large number of investors through direct sales alone. Looking at the experience of developed countries, direct sales only takes up around 10% of the total sales in the U.S. hedge funds.[9] As a lot of former public fund managers now work with privately offered fund companies, a number of investors follow. The reputations of the fund managers who are familiar with the market attract some investors to purchase fund products through direct sales.

Brokerages

As a sales channel of privately offered funds, brokerages recommend privately offered fund products to their own clients. Privately offered fund companies promise a certain trade volume to guarantee the commission income of brokerages. In recent years, brokerages have become more active in selling privately offered fund products as the competition between individual brokers has been very intense. The commission fees for independent brokers are falling, but institutional clients are constantly paying commission fees. Brokerages are willing to make fund products their major business. Furthermore, the clients of brokerages, especially the high-end ones, are no longer satisfied with only investing in stocks. Their demand of alternative high-return financial products is mounting.

To privately offered funds, brokerages can provide professional research reports for them. The risk-bearing ability of the clients of brokerages is usually high. They are more suited to the investment styles of privately offered funds.

Third-party financial management

Third-party financial institutions refer to independent intermediary financial institutions. They do not represent fund companies, banks, or insurance companies. They analyze the individual financial situation and needs for clients based on actual conditions. They utilize a variety of financial instruments in financial plans. Third-party financial institutions target the HNWIs in China. Sunshine private funds are one of the investment targets of third-party financial institutions. By selling sunshine private fund products to clients, they can receive subscription fees from the fund companies. They may even receive part of the fixed administration fees or investment returns from fund companies if the sales are of a considerable volume.

Thanks to its unique investment scope, differentiated investment styles, a reasonable risk-return relationship, and outstanding performance, sunshine private funds have become a major financial product of third-party financial institutions. During 2007–2008, third-party financial institutions contributed 30% to the sales of sunshine private funds.[10] In recent years, the development of third-party financial institutions has been promising. Those with larger market shares, such as Noah Private Wealth Management and Howbuy, can underwrite high-quality privately offered fund products. Looking at the experience of the U.S., the potential of third-party financial institutions is great. Although the situation in China is not as favorable, the legal system is being refined and the capital market is maturing. Third-party financial institutions will continue to grow, so will the sales of sunshine private funds.

Banks

The banks which sell privately offered fund products are mainly private commercial banks. Those banks offer a variety of financial services, including securities investment funds, insurance, financial derivatives, real estate, foreign exchange, gold, tax, venture capital, and legal advice. The also devise financial plans for individuals or families. After several years of exploration, private banks in China have developed to a considerable extent.

Having private banks as a sales channel is advantageous not only because of the overlapping in target customers, but also because the fund company can capitalize on the clients' trust in the private banks' professional financial services. The source of funds would be more stable.

Compared to public funds, privately offered fund products are more diverse, and both the risk and return are higher. Private banks can make more diverse financial plans tailored to individual clients. After 2008, the performance of sunshine private funds was outstanding and their investment styles became more consistent. In September 2009, the private banking department of the China Merchants Bank launched Chongyang 3 and raised RMB1.15 billion. The amount of funds was larger than the IPO of public funds at that time. This sparked interest in having private banks as a sales channel of sunshine private funds. Later, private banks have achieved favorable performances through sunshine private fund products such as Chongyang 5. The potential of the private banks sector to grow as a sales channel of privately offered funds is immense.

Facing challenges with innovation

Privately offered funds have encountered some challenges during their rapid development. The operation cost is rising and the difficulties in investment have intensified.

In the face of these two challenges, privately offered funds actively encourage innovations. There are limited partnership products and TOTs. They are the new developments of the industry.

Limited partnership products

Limited partnership has long been the prevalent form of operation of foreign hedge funds. In China, limited partnership sunshine private funds only began developing when the opening of trust accounts was suspended in July 2009 and when *Measures for the Administration of Securities Registration and Clearing* allowed limited partnership companies to open securities accounts. Traditional sunshine private funds operate through the platform of trust companies (See Fig. 6.42).

Fig. 6.42   Operation model of sunshine private funds

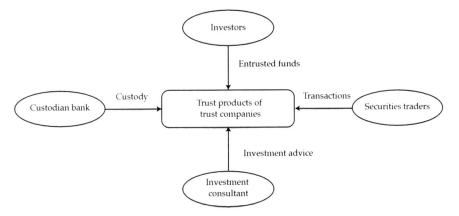

Limited partnership sunshine private funds are bound by the *Partnership Enterprise Law*. The general partner (fund management company) and no more than 49 limited partners (investors) establish the fund. The investors bear limited liability. The fund management company bears unlimited liability for the operation and debts of the fund. There are two operation models of limited partnership sunshine private funds (See Fig. 6.43).

The disadvantage of the first operation model 1 with 49 or fewer limited partners is that the funds raised may be constrained. The second operation model is the limited partnership and trust model. This is the prevalent operation model at present. Investors purchase the trust plans. As the trustee, the trust plan acts as a limited partner of a limited partnership fund. There are no constraints on the funds raised. This also reduces the tax burden on limited partnership companies as trust companies or foreign investments of trust products do not incur income tax.

Fig. 6.43   Operation models of limited partnership sunshine private funds

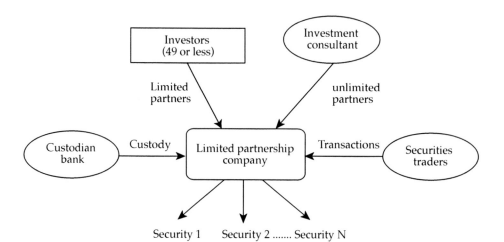

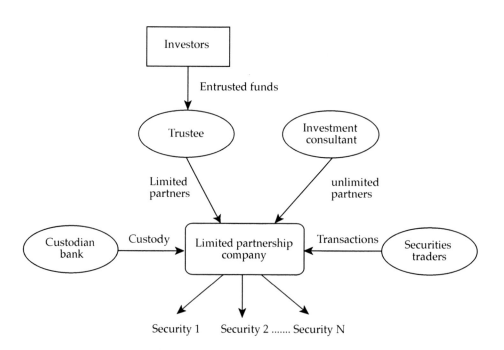

Limited partnership sunshine private funds avoid the problem of the suspension of the opening of securities accounts by trust companies. This reduces the cost of more than RMB1 million account fees and therefore lowers the cost of launching a product. The launch of a new product would not be hampered by the trust companies' requirements for the amount funds raised. The regulations stipulated in the *Regulations for the Administration of Futures Trading* do not restrict limited partnership companies from engaging in stock index futures trading. Sunshine private funds can adopt hedging strategies and become actual hedge funds.

Since the launch of Galaxy Purun — the first limited partnership sunshine private funds — in 2010, there have been more than 30 limited partnership sunshine private funds established in the market. The rapid development can be a breakthrough in the expansion of sunshine private funds.

Trusts of trusts

Trusts of trusts are an innovation of privately offered funds. The trust company set up a trust fund and raises funds. It chooses a privately offered fund company to be the investment manager to establish a trust, whose investment behaviors are restricted and monitored by the trust company. Through division of labor and specialization, the pursuit of absolute returns and risk diversification can be achieved.

TOT borrowed the idea from foreign funds of hedge funds (FOHF). Compared with sunshine private funds, TOT products are not restricted by the accounts of the trust companies. They alleviate the disequilibrium in the market. Other advantages of TOT include diversified investments, low investment threshold, having multiple regulators, and greater information disclosure.

In foreign markets, the growth rates of the quantity and AUM of FOHF products are higher than those of mutual funds and hedge funds. In China, the growth rate of TOT is astounding. Since May 2009, when China Ping An Trust launched the first TOT in China, Donghai Shengshi No.1 Collective Trust Funds, 53 more TOT have been launched in two years' time.

Despite the advantages mentioned above, at the present stage, the investment scope of TOT is small and only covers trusts. There is also double charging. Investment management is still in the exploratory stage. TOT focus on risk management and are more conservative in terms of investment.

There are other types of innovative sunshine private fund products. In 2011, privately placed products were popular in the market. The semi-structured sunshine private fund in China is also in preparation. Semi-structured sunshine private funds are a combination of structured and unstructured products. They evolve as an attempt to gain a breakthrough in the privately offered fund industry.

New features in 2011

The lifecycle theory states that an industry always experiences the stages of introduction, growth, maturity, and decline. The sunshine private fund industry is in the stage of having the high growth rates of the market and high demand, and this increases product variety and quantity. Problems are not uncommon during the transition period from one stage to another. The growing industry is facing challenges as it moves into the maturation stage. In the first half of 2011, issues such as liquidation, distribution, and mergers and acquisitions surfaced. The situation has never been more complicated.

As of May 2011, 11 sunshine private fund products had been liquidated. There are several reasons why the sunshine private fund products were liquidated: the fund managers voluntarily wrapped up operations; it was the end of the funds' duration or the funds matured; investors withdrew which reduced the size of the fund to the extent that liquidation becomes necessary; or the unit value of the product dropped below the stop-loss line which necessitated compulsory liquidation. In January 2008, Zhao Danyang voluntary liquidated SZITIC Pure Heart China Investment Trust. Zhao claimed that under the market conditions, there was no investment target which matched his investment criteria or which had an adequate margin of safety. It was a classic case of a fund manager voluntary winding up a fund, which is uncommon in China. Zhao's action is considered by the industry an example of upholding the philosophy of value investing. The reasons of liquidation of the products during January to May 2011 are show in Table 6.11.

Of the 11 products above, 6 were liquidated due to the end of maturity. Springs Capital 1 was the only one that was liquidated because of poor business performance. Although Shenlan 1 suffered a loss of 33.93% when it was liquidated, the drop was not below the stop loss line. The size of Dinghongyi 1 was not large when it was launched. As investors withdrew, its size was reduced to a level that warranted liquidation. Aikang 1 and Xindongfang Growth were reorganized and acquired by other fund companies and therefore liquidated. From this analysis, it can be seen that although the performance of sunshine private funds were not satisfactory and performance differentiation was severe in the first five months of 2011, these were not the major reason for liquidation. Although there were cases of investor withdrawal, it was not a trend. Liquidation reduced the funds in the industry by RMB6 billion to RMB8 billion. The 378 new products launched in the first half of the year brought in RMB30 billion to RMB40 billion. It can be considered that the increase and decrease in funds is balanced out.

Table 6.11   Reasons for liquidation of 11 sunshine private fund products during January to May 2011

Product	Reason for liquidation	Product	Reason for liquidation
Menxiang 8	End of maturity	Shenlan 1	Compulsory liquidation
Yongsheng Huiyuan	End of maturity	Xindongfang Growth	Reorganized as Long-Term Investment 10
Yitai 3 (Structured product)	End of maturity	Aikang 1	Acquired by Dingfeng Assets and became Dingfeng 11
Huabao 1	End of maturity	Dinghongyi 1	The size of fund was too small
Tongwei 1	End of maturity	Springs Capital 1 (structured)	Compulsory liquidation as unit value dropped below stop loss line
Yili Dongfang	End of maturity		

Note: This information here focuses on unstructured products. In the first half of 2011, around 60 structured products were liquidated, mostly because of the end of maturity.

Source: Data from Wind Info analyzed by the Private Fund Research Center of Hua Ming Chuangfu Fund (HMC Fund).

Also, sunshine private funds have a greater pressure to maintain their size. Although the number of issuance of sunshine private products in the first half of 2011 was greater than that over the same period in 2010, the issue size was in fact smaller. Mergers and acquisitions of sunshine private funds mentioned above took place because of the small product size, to a large extent.

The reorganization of Aikang 1 and Xindongfang Growth were a manifestation of the unspoken rules of the sunshine private fund industry: The size of some older products is small. It was difficult for them to pay certain fees. Privately offered fund companies may acquire the shell resources of these low-return smaller funds. New products are launched using the trust accounts of those older products to save costs. In the first half of 2011, Cheetah 1, Cheetah 2, and Chuangying 1 were acquired by or merged with other sunshine private funds. As more "underground" privately offered funds are hoping to become legal sunshine private funds, smaller funds which have business difficulties are at a higher chance of being acquired or merged.

The pressure on the size of the funds not only leads to the liquidation of some older funds but also difficulties in launching new fund products. In 2011, there was the first failure of launch of sunshine private funds. According to Simuwang, the launch of 16 products was postponed, including products of Shanghai Elegant Investment Co., Ltd., and YCT Investment Management Co., Ltd. The reasons behind are mainly poor business performances or the size requirement by trust companies has become larger. The threshold for launching new products was raised.

In order to expand the scale, privately offered funds invested more resources in sales. Expanding sales channels such as partnering with private banks incur increasingly high costs. If the year-end return of a privately offered fund is 20%, it is estimated that 60% of the administration fee of the fund would go to the private bank. With a lower rate of return, the fund company may even suffer losses. At present, the size of funds can grow to RMB100 billion in a short period of time, and the annual issuance can amount to more than RMB10 billion. The costs of sales are over RMB1 billion. The change in competition strategies aggravates the sales pressure of the fund companies. This poses potential problems. It is possible that the "size-first" competition strategy would make privately offered funds focus on the competition among charges and fees like public funds and neglect other aspects. This is a concern of the industry.

As competition becomes more keen, the problems with human resources surface. According to Simuwang, in the first half of 2011, there are at least eight fund managers who have tendered their resignation. The turnover rate of researchers is also high. As fund managers leave public funds for privately offered funds, there are those who change from companies to companies or from privately offered funds to public funds. As the AUM of privately offered funds grow, the companies' demand for researchers increases. Employees of a company may be recruited by other companies. Also, the difference in investment philosophy or strategies is a reason behind the flow of talents. As the performance of privately offered funds drops, researchers may look for public fund companies for a more stable income and greater security.

Challenges are inevitable during the development of an industry. After several years, sunshine private funds experienced the difficulties in the transition from the stages of growth to maturation. Poor business performance, liquidation, and mergers and acquisitions are precursors to a reshuffling of the industry. As competition becomes fiercer, the principle of the survival of the fittest will eliminate weak privately offered funds. The concentration of the industry will increase.

7

Chapter

Analysis of the Current Situation of China's Private Securities Investment Fund Companies

This chapter studies the top 100 sunshine private funds based on the data of Wind Info as of May 31, 2011. The list is shown in Table 7.7. We analyze the features and development trends of sunshine private fund companies from the perspective of management structure, team building, and products. In terms of the management structure, the organization of privately offered fund companies is gradually being regulated, the decision-making process is more rigorous, and the companies are paying more attention to risk-control. As for team building, the companies assemble a team with high-quality and diversified investment styles. In terms of products, the companies favor floating structured products with a guarantee and hybrid unstructured products.

Features of the Management of Private Securities Investment Fund Companies

In the early development stage of the majority of private securities investment fund companies, the operation was unregulated and the organizational structure was inadequate. Decisions were mostly made by only one person instead of a team. Some companies did not have an internal risk-control system. As the privately offered fund industry developed, it transitioned from a period without regulation to an era of regulation. Privately offered fund companies, especially sunshine private fund companies, have become more regulated. Most of them adopt a U-shape and flat organizational structure. The decision-making process is more meticulous and companies are more concerned about internal risk-control.

Gradual regulation of the organization of fund companies

Typical U-shape organizational structure of sunshine private fund companies

According to the company websites, the top 100 sunshine private fund companies by product scale all have a linear organizational structure, which is also called a U-shape organizational structure. The U-shape structure is the unitary structure. The management exercise centralized control. There is also the M-shape (Multidivisional) structure, in which management is decentralized.

In the U-shape structure, different functional departments are under the leadership of top management. This organizational structure is suitable for companies that produce a single product, employ few employees, and have little decision-making information. Privately offered fund companies have all the above features. By adopting a U-shape structure, private securities investment fund companies can increase the incentive of the employees and lower the management costs, which are beneficial for the operation of the companies. The typical organizational structure of sunshine private fund companies is shown in Fig. 7.1.

Fig.7.1   **Typical organizational structure of sunshine private fund companies**

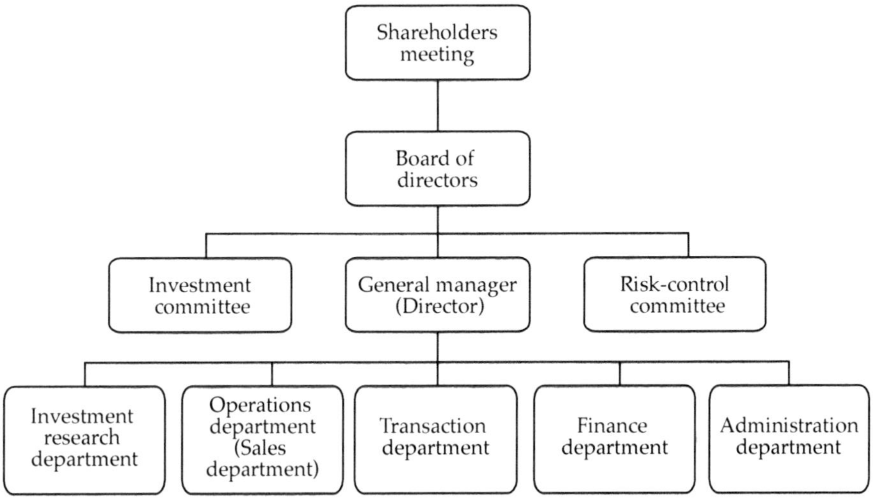

Source: Private Fund Research Center of Hua Ming Chuangfu Fund (HMC Fund).

Features of the organizational structure of sunshine private fund companies

Compared to public fund companies, securities companies, and trust companies, the structure of the sunshine private fund companies is the simplest. This is related to the features of the companies. Sunshine private fund companies target a small number of select investors. They have a need for operational flexibility. A simple U-shape structure is adequate for the needs of the companies. A complicated organizational structure would hamper the development of the companies. The comparison of the structures of sunshine private fund companies and other financial institutions are shown in Table 7.1.

Table 7.1   Comparison of the structure of sunshine private fund companies and other financial institutions

Sunshine private fund companies	Other financial institutions
Linear functional organizational structure	Organizational structure with functional departments, subsidiaries, divisions
Centered on investment research, other departments are supporting	Balanced structure and departmental status
In small companies, the specialization of department is not enough. Investment and investment research are usually conducted by the same department, and transaction department is not separated.	Individual investment department, investment research department, and transaction department
Companies with a public fund background pay more attention to sales, other companies are less concerned about assembling a sales team	Pay attention to marketing and sales channels
Flexible operation and sensitive to the market	Less flexible operation and less sensitive to the market

Source: Private Fund Research Center of Hua Ming Chuangfu Fund (HMC Fund).

After years of development, the organizational structure of sunshine private fund companies is becoming more standardized. In the next step, the companies should carry out structural adjustment: The structure should center on the investment research department. More attention should be given to marketing and sales and risk-control. The companies should implement these adjustments so as to survive the next industry reshuffle.

Flat hierarchical organizational structure

Definition of hierarchy

In management, there are two common parameters in the analysis of hierarchy: management range and management levels. Management range is also called management width. It refers to the number of departments or subordinates under the management of the manager of a particular level. Management levels refer to the number of levels of managers in the position chain.

Management range and management levels are in an inverse relationship. A company with a wider management range has fewer management levels, and vice versa. It should be noted that in classic management theories, there is a most suitable hierarchical structure corresponding to different types of companies. For a smaller management range and more management levels, it is a tall hierarchy. For a larger management range and fewer management levels, it is a flat hierarchy.

The features of a flat hierarchy are as follows:
- Convenient communication between decision-making levels and operations level; orders executed quickly and precisely
- Few managers with litter bureaucracy; low administration fee
- Encouragement of subordinates to take initiative and be active

Analysis of the current situation and advantages of the organizational structure of sunshine private fund companies

For sunshine private fund companies, the number of management levels is usually smaller than four and the management range is smaller than five people. Some larger companies have an investment research team of more than 10 members under the management of the head of the team. This shows that sunshine private fund companies have a flat organizational structure.

To privately offered fund companies, especially sunshine private fund companies, a flat organizational structure has the following advantages over a tall organizational structure: First, the investors of sunshine private funds do not want common, mass-produced, unitary, or standard products. They want unique, diversified, and personalized fund products tailored to their needs. A tall hierarchical structure is not as flexible as a flat structure to suit the needs of the investors.

Second, sunshine private fund companies cannot rely on mass production to gain scale advantages. The companies need to shorten the time spend on product development and produce products tailored to the needs of the investors. A flat hierarchical structure is more sensitive to the market demand and therefore more advantageous.

Third, due to rapid development of information technology, social mobility increases. There is significantly increased activity among social organizations. The changing market and fleeting opportunities induce huge pressure on the fund companies to react more quickly to maintain the vitality of enterprises. The customer-oriented and decentralized flat hierarchical structure is more suitable for the development of the privately offered fund companies.

Compared to public fund companies, there are fewer management levels in sunshine private fund companies. As sunshine private fund companies also employ fewer people than public fund companies, their management range is also smaller. As the optimal structure is specific to each type of company, there is not a better structure in this comparison. It is, however, certain that the majority of sunshine private fund companies adopt a flat structure to suit their own development.

More meticulous decision-making process

The typical investment decision-making process of sunshine private fund companies is shown in Fig. 7.2.

Fig. 7.2   **Typical investment decision-making process of sunshine private fund companies**

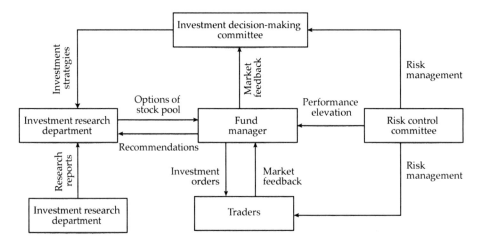

Source: Private Fund Research Center of Hua Ming Chuangfu Fund (HMC Fund).

First, the investment decision-making committee determines the investment style and strategies. Decisions are made based on market analysis, the requirement of risk-control, and expected return. The overall investment plan is formulated or adjusted.

Second, the investment team has to come up with options of stock pools and investment recommendations. A stock pool is formed after research and approval.

Third, the fund manager builds an investment portfolio based on investment decisions and the stock pool. In the actual investment process, fund managers are under the supervision of the risk-control committee. They reflect the market feedback to the investment decision-making committee.

Fourth, the fund manager passes investment orders to traders. Traders operate individually. Individuality is ensured to avoid operational risk.

As the above four processes are underway at the same time, the risk-control committee should supervise closely the investment behavior and evaluate the performance of the fund manager. Through monitoring the investment decision-making process and the execution of investment orders, the committee formulates the risk-control policies for real-time stock prices in the market and makes relevant recommendations. The typical stock selection process of sunshine private fund companies is shown in Fig. 7.3.

Fig. 7.3   Typical stock selection process of sunshine private fund companies

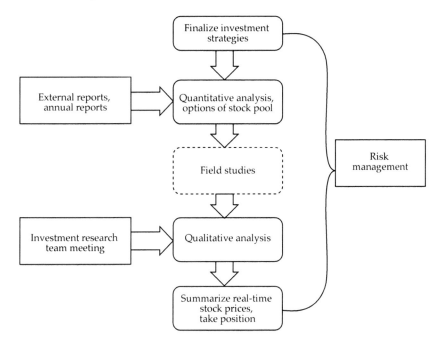

Source: Private Fund Research Center of Hua Ming Chuangfu Fund (HMC Fund).

After several years of development, the decision-making process of sunshine private fund companies has been well-established. It shows the following features:

Collective decision-making is usually adopted. It is more scientific than individual decision-making was in the past. Research is conducted as a team rather than by individuals.

Compared to the past, security is now a greater concern in the decision-making process. Risk control in every step is strictly implemented. Investments are now safer. The decision-making process of large sunshine private fund companies is similar to that of public fund companies. One of the disadvantages of sunshine private fund companies is the small number of researchers. However, as the companies expand, this disadvantage would be reduced. The decision-making process would become more meticulous.

Privately offered fund companies pay increasingly more attention to risk management

Nonsystematic risk specific to privately offered fund companies

Given the private securities investment fund companies' unique features and investment environment, apart from the systematic risk in the capital market, they are also under nonsystematic risk, including legal risk, credit risk, operational risk, and liquidity risk.

Legal risk

The main legal risk of private securities investment companies is the lack of legal status. Privately offered fund companies have always been marginalized by the law. They have yet to obtain legal status. Their development is restrained, and it is difficult for the government to regulate the companies. According to Simuwang's *Report on China's Private Securities Funds for the First Six Months of 2011*, the lack of legal status is the primary obstacle to the development of private securities investment funds. Legalization and the establishment of sunshine private funds is the direction for the future development of the industry in China.[1]

Credit risk

Credit risk refers to the risk borne by investors if the private securities investment company fails to abide by the contract because of closing down or other reasons. The information on the operation of the companies is usually not disclosed. There is no regulation on information disclosure, which leads to information asymmetry between investors and fund managers. This is unfavorable for protecting the investors' interest. Without external constraints, the fund manager can maximize his own benefits and damage the interest of the investors. They can also conspire with the listed companies to conduct insider trading and price manipulation, exaggerate the expected rate of return, or make false promises. These can all cause a loss on the investors' part.

Operational risk

Operational risk refers to the risk if fund managers of private securities investment funds adopt illegal measures to manipulate the securities market in order to earn higher profits. Private securities investment funds can use high leverage. Fund managers usually use leverage to expand their size of funds in the hope of obtaining higher profits. However, due to the poor information disclosure system and loose government supervision, fund managers may attempt to manipulate the securities market using leverage. This increases the market risk.

Liquidity risk

Liquidity risk refers to the difficulties of cashing funds as the funds are invested in securities investment funds. In general, private securities investment funds have a certain locked-up period. In order to guarantee the sustainability and stability of the securities investment funds, the withdrawal of funds is prohibited. Moreover, unlike public funds, private securities investment funds cannot transfer risk or cash in their funds through the secondary market. This induces considerable liquidity risk. Investors may suffer from debt risk because of high liquidity risk.

Risk management system of sunshine private fund companies

The risk management system of sunshine private fund companies can be categorized into three types.

Internal risk control by the investment order

Investment is divided into three stages: before, in progress, and afterwards. Risk control is conducted specific to the stage of investment (See Fig. 7.4). Before making the actual investment, risk control focuses on the stock pool. During the actual investment, risk-control focuses on the isolation of fund managers and traders in order to minimize operational risk of human error. The profit stop mechanism is effective at this stage. After the investment is made, performance review and compliance management are conducted for future reference.

Fig.7.4   Internal risk control by the investment order

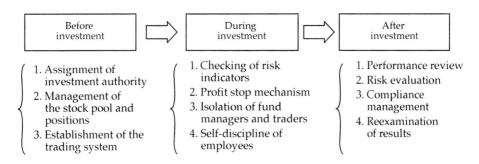

Internal risk control by department

Under this system, risk-control is specific to the nature of the department (See Fig. 7.5). However, constrained by the size, a lot of privately offered fund companies do not create the position of director of research. Research is directed by the director of investment. Some companies even lack traders. Trading is conducted directly by fund managers.

Fig. 7.5   Internal risk control by department

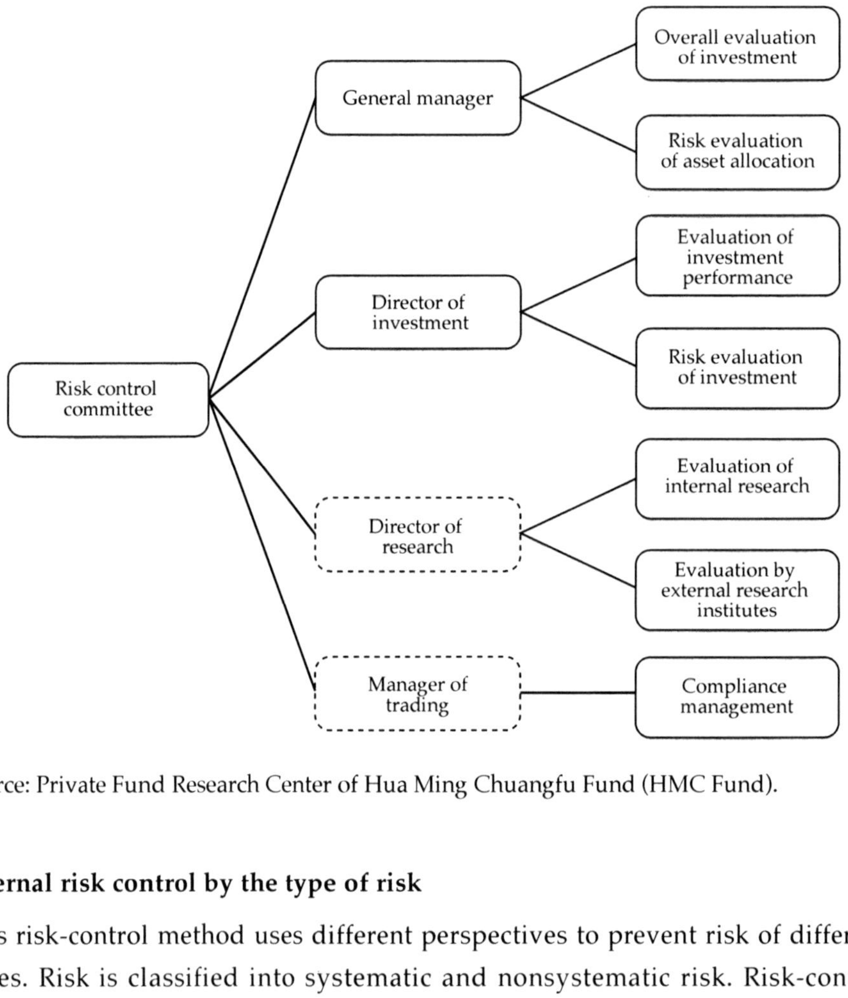

Source: Private Fund Research Center of Hua Ming Chuangfu Fund (HMC Fund).

Internal risk control by the type of risk

This risk-control method uses different perspectives to prevent risk of different types. Risk is classified into systematic and nonsystematic risk. Risk-control is conducted based on the features of the two types of risk (See Fig. 7.6). Some companies use the risk hedging mechanism to reduce the risk of the investment portfolio. As China's hedging mechanism is not well-established, few companies have adopted this mechanism.

Fig. 7.6   Internal risk control by the type of risk

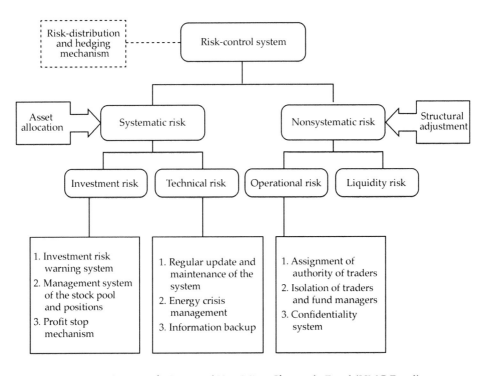

Source: Private Fund Research Center of Hua Ming Chuangfu Fund (HMC Fund).

One privately offered fund product was chosen from the three different types of risk-control methods as the subjects of our study. Their downside risk in the past year is shown in Table 7.2. It can be seen that apart from Product B, the downside risk of the other two products was lower than that of public fund products. As analyzed in Section 2 of Chapter 6, from 2007 to 2010, the average downside risk of sunshine private fund products was lower than that of public fund products. Sunshine private funds showed greater ability in risk-control.

The data above shows that sunshine private fund companies are paying more and more attention to risk-control. Investors can have faith in their products.

There is an area waiting for improvement and refinement in the risk-control system of the sunshine private fund companies. As most sunshine private fund companies only employ one fund manager, who may be the central figure of the company and the leader of the investment research team, this centralization of authority can pose problems in the prevention of nonsystematic risk. Sunshine private fund companies can only improve the situation by expanding the team and decentralize authority as they continue to develop.

Table 7.2   Downside risk of selected fund products

	Product	Downside risk (past one year)	Downside risk (since establishment)
Internal risk control by the investment order	Privately offered fund product A	0.25	0.22
Internal risk control by department	Privately offered fund product B	0.34	0.29
Internal risk control by the type of risk	Privately offered fund product C	0.22	0.22
	Public fund products	0.29	—

Note: The data is as of May 31, 2011.

Source: Data from Wind Info analyzed by the Private Fund Research Center of Hua Ming Chuangfu Fund (HMC Fund).

Features of the Human Talent in Private Securities Investment Fund Companies

This section analyzes the central figures and investment research teams of the privately offered fund companies. The employees are of high quality and have diversified investment styles. Despite that, the companies are lagging behind in team building and personnel training and the cost of human resources is affecting the companies' development, the future of the companies looks promising under the strategy of centering on human resources.

Central figure with diversified investment styles

The central figure of private securities investment fund companies is usually the director or general manager. The person is the key management personnel of the company. In investment-led privately offered fund companies, the person is also the general manager of investment. The history of private securities investment funds in China is short. The central figure is usually the founder of the fund, whose behavior can determine the development of the company.

The top 50 sunshine private fund companies by product size according to Wind Info have been chosen for this study. The features of the central figure, including the number of fund products he/she manages, background, education, and professional experience are analyzed. The information is as of May 31, 2011.

Number of fund products the central figure manages

The central figures of China's sunshine private fund companies manage an average 68% of the number of products or amount of assets of the companies. Their decision-making is directly related to the performance of the products and the profits of the company. Any action of theirs can affect the future development of the company.

The central figures usually manage operating fund products. Only 10% of the central figures do not manage fund products. This shows that their main responsibility is to make investments. To privately offered fund companies, investment research is more important than marketing and sales management. It is natural that the central figures value investment research more. The majority of companies center on the investment research team. Other departments are supporting.

Background of the central figures

Features of central figures with different backgrounds

In the early period of China's capital market, some manipulators or agents formed the prototype of privately offered funds through "offices" or "rat trading." These financial practitioners were called grassroots practitioners. As private securities investment fund companies expand, some employees of large securities companies or brokerages change industry to work in private securities investment fund companies. Around 2007, some public fund managers entered the industry of privately offered funds. There are also fund managers with a background in banking, trust companies, or insurance companies. Some conducted industrial investment or worked in financial media organizations.

As shown in Fig. 7.8, of the top 50 privately offered fund companies by size, the percentage of the central figures with different backgrounds is in this order: brokerage, public fund, others, and grassroots. The percentage of former brokerage employees or former public fund managers was similar. Together they contributed to 70%. This shows that as the capital market becomes more regulated, former brokerage employees and former public fund managers can more easily succeed with a well-established regulatory system and investment processes. Privately offered fund companies are becoming more regulated.

Fig. 7.7   Central figures and the products their manage

Number of products a central figure manages

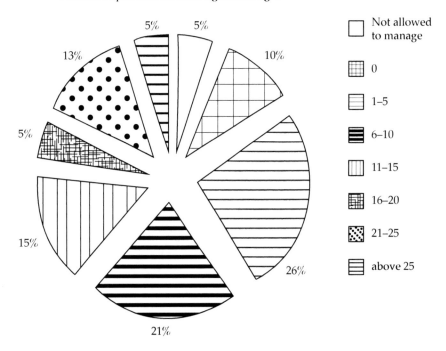

Legend	
☐	Not allowed to manage
▦	0
▤	1–5
▬	6–10
▥	11–15
▦	16–20
▨	21–25
▤	above 25

	Number of products managed by the central figure	Percentage of number of products managed by the central figure in terms of total product (%)
Mean	9.62	0.68
Median	8.00	0.88
Smallest value	0.00	0.00
Largest value	34.00	1.00

Source: Data from Wind Info analyzed by the Private Fund Research Center of Hua Ming Chuangfu Fund (HMC Fund) and various company websites.

Although fund managers of certain backgrounds are more common in the privately offered fund industry, there is no strong preference for a certain investment style. Diversified and personalized investment styles can develop in the industry, which is a unique feature of the industry. For public funds, due to institutional constraints and inadequacies of the incentive mechanism, the investment style of the central figure is not diversified.

Fig. 7.8   Features of the central figures of different backgrounds

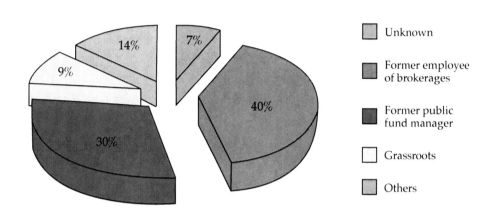

Unknown

Former employee of brokerages

Former public fund manager

Grassroots

Others

Source: Data from Wind Info analyzed by the Private Fund Research Center of Hua Ming Chuangfu Fund (HMC Fund).

Analysis of different investment styles

Thanks to a different background, the central figures have their own investment style and philosophy. This contributes to the diversified investment styles of privately offered fund companies.

(1) Former employees of brokerages
As most of them were former researchers, they pay more attention to research on individual stocks and prefer a higher degree of ownership concentration.

(2) Former public fund managers
They are more concerned about the investment research process and sales services. First, they disclose information on a regular basis. The net asset value and other information are publicized in quarterly and annual reports. The transparency of business performance is the highest priority.

    Second, there are strict regulations on the investment research process. Internal management is adequate.

    Third, they pay more attention to sales channels and customer services.
(3) Grassroots financial practitioners
The grassroots fund managers have more experience in making investment in the securities market. They are more apt at market operations and have more

diversified investment styles. The frequency of switching stocks is usually higher. They pay more attention to the technical analysis of stocks.

(4) Others

The other fund managers come from financial institutions including banks, trust companies, and insurance companies. Some have conducted industrial investment or worked in financial media organizations. They have ventured into the privately offered fund industry in recent years. The number is relatively small.

Over all, in the face of multi-layered financial demand, diversification and differentiation in the investment styles would allow privately offered funds to develop alongside public funds.

Features of the educational and professional background of central figures

Educational background

In privately offered fund companies, more than half of the central figures hold a master's degree. Some even hold a doctorate degree (See Fig. 7.9). The situation is similar to public fund companies.

Fig. 7.9   **Educational background of the central figures of sunshine private fund companies**

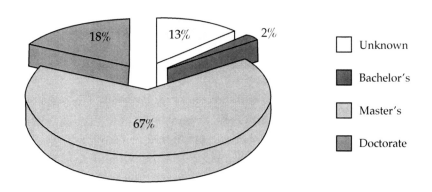

Sources: Wind Info, Simuwang, Private Fund Research Center of Hua Ming Chuangfu Fund (HMC Fund), and various company websites.

The central figures in sunshine private fund companies usually hold higher educational qualifications, similar to public fund companies. The companies are in high demand for highly educated, highly qualified personnel.

Professional background

Most of the central figures in sunshine private fund companies have an economics background (52%). Others have a background in management (14%), engineering (10%), science (8%), law (2%), and philosophy (2%) (See Fig. 7.10). Apart from having 52% of central figures having an economic background, the background for the others is quite diverse with a focus on science and engineering.

Industry experience

Of the central figures, 75% have more than 10 years of experience in the industry. The average years of experience is 13. The figures are familiar with the industry and have rich experience in asset management (See Fig. 7.11). Most of the fund managers of sunshine private funds are between 30 and 40 years of age. They are in the prime of their life. These two factors allow them to strive for better performance to bring in higher profits for the companies. This is similar to the situation of public fund companies.

Fig. 7.10   **Professional background of the central figures of sunshine private fund companies**

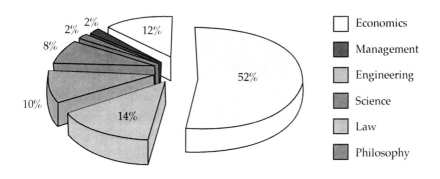

Sources: Wind Info, Simuwang, Private Fund Research Center of Hua Ming Chuangfu Fund (HMC Fund), and various company websites.

Fig. 7.11   Industry experience of the central figures of sunshine private fund companies

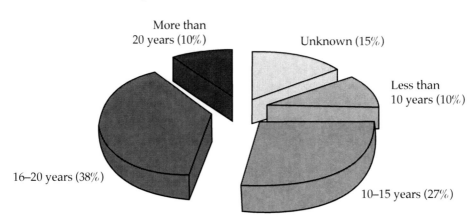

Unknown (15%), less than 10 years (10%), 10–15 years (27%), 16–20 years (38%), more than 20 years (10%)

Sources: Wind Info, Simuwang, Private Fund Research Center of Hua Ming Chuangfu Fund (HMC Fund), and various company websites.

Summarizing the above analyses, the common features of the central figures of sunshine private fund companies are large number of products under management, high educational level, and rich experience. These features are similar to those of the central figures in public fund companies. They are the elite in the industry. The differences with those in public fund companies are that they have more diversified and unique investment styles and philosophies. This is because of the greater flexibility given by the system of sunshine private funds and their personal background.

Investment research team waiting to be developed

The investment research team includes an investment decision-making committee, fund managers, researchers, and other personnel who are involved in investment decision-making. The size, proportion of female employees, and educational background of the investment research teams of the top 40 sunshine private fund companies by product size are analyzed below.

Size of the investment research team

The average number of members of the investment research teams of the top 40 companies is smaller than 10. The largest number is 17 and the smaller is 1, and

3 is the most common number of members. The proportions of companies with different numbers of members in the investment research teams are shown in Fig. 7.12. It can be seen that although the team is a core part of sunshine private fund companies, the number of members is small.

Fig. 7.12   **Proportion of companies with different number of members in the investment research team**

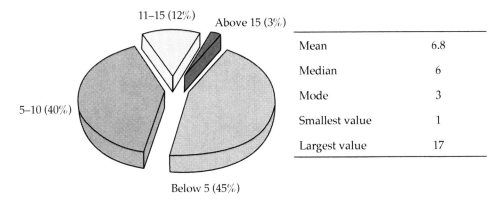

Mean	6.8
Median	6
Mode	3
Smallest value	1
Largest value	17

Sources: Wind Info, Private Fund Research Center of Hua Ming Chuangfu Fund (HMC Fund), and various company websites.

The number of members in investment research is generally lower in sunshine private fund companies than in public fund companies. The number in fast-growing and large sunshine private fund companies is only comparable to that of small public fund companies.

At present, the size of investment research teams in sunshine private funds is small. However, as the industry grows and the number of sunshine private fund companies increases, the number of products and asset size would also increase. The research teams would expand.

Proportion of female members

The difference of perspective between men and women can increase the efficiency in operation and management. Having female members can bring in different ideas, which can help lower the risk.

In the top 40 sunshine private fund companies, the proportion of female members in the investment research team is 12.39%. The average number of female members is 0.85. In 57% of the companies, there are no female members. There are 5 and 3 female members in 5% and 3% of the companies, respectively (See Fig. 7.13).

Fig. 7.13 Proportion of female members in the investment research team of sunshine private fund companies

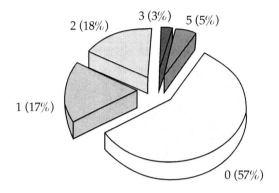

	Number of female members	Proportion of female members
Mean	0.85	0.12
Median	0	0
Mode	0	0
Smallest value	0	0
Largest value	5	0.83

Sources: Wind Info, Private Fund Research Center of Hua Ming Chuangfu Fund (HMC Fund), and various company websites.

Some sunshine private fund companies do not see a need to being in more female members to the investment research team. This shows that further development is needed for the team.

Educational background

Researchers of privately offered fund companies hold at least a bachelor's degree. The majority hold a master's degree (including MBA and EMBA). Some hold a doctorate degree. As shown in Fig. 7.14, privately offered fund companies are in high demand for high quality personnel. The lack of doctorate researchers is a roadblock for the development of the investment research teams of these companies.

Through the above analyses, it can be seen that he development of the investment research teams of sunshine private fund companies is slightly lagging behind the development of public fund companies. However, the average quality of team members is higher in sunshine private fund companies. A lot of trustworthy investment research teams have been established. In terms of the size and the proportion of female members, sunshine private fund companies have to catch up with public fund companies. The development of the investment research team in sunshine private fund companies cannot match the growth of the company. The investment research teams still have much room for development.

Fig. 7.14   **Educational background of the central figures of sunshine private fund companies**

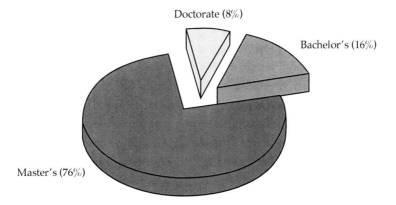

Sources: Wind Info, Private Fund Research Center of Hua Ming Chuangfu Fund (HMC Fund), and various company websites.

Development bottleneck: Lack of human resources

Development strategies centered on human resources

Since 2007, the sunshine private fund industry has achieved unprecedented success. The number of new products continues to grow rapidly. However, the recruitment and nurturing of talents has not been as fast, especially for researchers.

Compared to the investment research teams of public fund companies with more than 30 members, around 61% of sunshine private fund companies only have a team of 5 to 10 members. Very few teams have more than 20 members. In addition, the majority of sunshine private fund companies only have 10 to 20 employees. Few employ more than 30 people. There are usually only 1 to 2 fund managers. This shows that privately offered fund companies are at a bottleneck in terms of the recruitment of talents.

To privately offered fund companies, team building and personnel training are core elements for their development. These companies are building their brand and trying to win the trust of their investors. They want to recruit people who are familiar with the market and have experience in asset management. At present, the companies are generally in need of researchers. They should formulate their development strategies with a focus on human resources, building their research and sales teams. They should adopt a training system to nurture their employees in order to maintain sustainability.

Now, some privately offered fund companies have realized the importance of human resources. In the face of the limited supply of human talent, the companies have formulated incentive mechanisms such as equity rewards, bonuses, opportunities for promotion, vacations, and air tickets for visiting relatives in order to retain the high quality personnel. Some sunshine private fund companies offer target-oriented personnel training, especially for researchers. They recruit employees at school and provide opportunities for further studies or internal learning.

It can be expected that the maturing of China's capital market, especially the opening up of the stock index futures market, would stimulate the growth of privately offered fund companies. The quickly expanding companies are in demand for not only more personnel, but also personnel of higher quality. They would prefer the fund managers to have an investment style similar to the higher management of the company and researchers to have relevant working experience rather than education in economics or finance only. The companies may need more time and effort to build and nurture a team of professionals.

It is a new phenomenon after large sunshine private fund companies are established that large companies attract the personnel and customers of small companies. An industry reshuffling is becoming more imminent.

Constraint of development by overly high cost of human resources

In recent years, the market has had an increasing demand for researchers, but the supply is limited. The salary of researchers has risen to a high level, which incurs a higher cost of human resources for the companies.

To sunshine private fund companies, especially the small ones, the increasingly high cost of human resources is an obstacle. The size of the companies is usually small. They do not hold any advantage in offering salary or position compared to large public fund companies.

For example, when a sunshine private fund company launches a product of RMB100 million with a rate of return of 20%, even in the perfect situation in which the trust company is not involved in the allocation of floating profit, the company can only obtain RMB4 million. Deducting the operation costs and rent, there are no funds to support an investment research team. Additionally, few sunshine private funds can obtain a rate of return of 20%.

As of the end of May 2011, the average rate of return on sunshine private funds in the previous year was only 4.63%. Unless all fund products of the companies can raise more than RMB10 billion, they cannot maintain normal operation and bear the high cost of human resources. This is an inevitable obstacle in the development of small privately offered fund companies. In their early development, they were only able to launch one fund product which raised around RMB100 million. Their profit was limited and therefore they did not have enough funds to attract high quality personnel. The size of the funds raised by public funds is huge, and the companies receive stable administration fees. Their stable profit and financial power allow them to bear the high cost of human resources.

In conclusion, for growth privately offered fund companies, their human resource power is lagging behind. This is caused by the lack of talents and the high cost of human resources. Small and uncompetitive sunshine private fund companies may be liquidated. Larger companies may grasp the opportunity to develop. The problem with human resources is an obstacle that privately offered funds must tackle. Those which can overcome the problem should have an improvement in quality.

Features of the Products of Private Securities Investment Fund Companies

This section analyzes the rate structure and the profit sharing ratio of some private securities investment fund products, in particular sunshine private fund products.

The top 10 privately offered fund companies by product size were chosen as subjects of this study (See Table 7.3). The features of the top 10 fund products by the cumulative rate of return of over a period of three years are shown in Table 7.4.

Table 7.3   Features of the top 10 sunshine private fund products (%)

Product	Front-end fee	Administration fee	Redemption fee	Profit sharing ratio
Elegant 1	1	1.50	No redemption in the first six months; 3% redemption fee during 6–12 months; no redemption fee after 12 months	20

Table 7.3   Features of the top 10 sunshine private fund products (%)

(Cont'd)

Product	Front-end fee	Administration fee	Redemption fee	Profit sharing ratio
Rosefinch 1	1	1.50	No redemption in the first six months; 3% redemption fee during 6–12 months; no redemption fee after 12 months	20
StarRock 1	1	1.50	3% redemption fee during 7–12 months; no redemption fee after 12 months	20
Springs Capital Growth 1	1	1.55	5% redemption fee under 12 months; no redemption fee after 12 months	20
Congrong Advantage 1	1	2.00	5% within lock-up period; no redemption fee after lock-up period	20
China Dragon 1	1	1.20	One to two years: 0.8% Two to three years: 0.4% Three to four years: 0.2% Above four years: 0%	20
Wudang 1	1	1.50	3% redemption fee during 6–12 months; no redemption fee after 12 months	20
Bohong Placement Index 3	1	1.20	—	20% of the annualized rate of return excluding the first 6%
Huili Preferred 1	1	2.20	—	20
StarRock 3	1	1.70	No redemption fee after lock-up period	20

Notes: (i) Administration fee includes fund administration fee and custodian fee.
(ii) The product was either being promoted on their website or the first or the second product they launched.

Sources: Wind Info, Simuwang, and various company websites.

Table 7.4   Features of the top 10 fund products by the cumulative rate of return of over a period of three years (%)

Product	Front-end fee	Administration fee	Redemption fee	Profit sharing ratio
Elegant 4	1	1.50	No redemption in the first six months; 3% redemption fee during 6 to 12 months; no redemption fee after 12 months	20
Elegant 3	1	1.50	No redemption in the first six months; 3% redemption fee during 6 to 12 months; no redemption fee after 12 months	20
Lonteng	1	1.50	No redemption in the first six months; 3% redemption fee during 6 to 12 months; no redemption fee after 12 months	20
Shitong 1	1	1.50	No redemption in the first six months; 3% redemption fee during 6 to 12 months; no redemption fee after 12 months	20
Shitong 1	1	1.50	No redemption in the first six months; 3% redemption fee during 6 to 12 months; no redemption fee after 12 months	20
New Value 2 (Guangdong Finance)	1	1.50	(1) No redemption during lock-up period, but not applicable to trust funds which are directly converted from the profit of the trust plan (2) No redemption fee after lock-up period	20
New Value 3	1	1.50	(1) No redemption during lock-up period, but not applicable to trust funds which are directly converted from the profit of the trust plan (2) No redemption fee after lock-up period	20

Table 7.4   **Features of the top 10 fund products by the cumulative rate of return of over a period of three years (%)**

(Cont'd)

Product	Front-end fee	Administration fee	Redemption fee	Profit sharing ratio
Rosefinch 2 (SZITIC)	1	1.50	No redemption in the first six months; 3% redemption fee during 6 to 12 months; no redemption fee after 12 months	20
Springs Capital 2008	1	1.55	5% redemption in the first 12 months; no redemption fee after 12 months	20
Rosefinch 1 (SZITIC)	1	1.50	No redemption in the first six months; 3% redemption fee during 6 to 12 months; no redemption fee after 12 months	20
Elegant 1 (SZITIC)	1	1.50	No redemption in the first six months; 3% redemption fee during 6 to 12 months; no redemption fee after 12 months	20

Note: Administration fee includes fund administration fee and custodian fee.

Sources: Wind Info, Simuwang, and various company websites.

Rate structure of products

When investors invest in fund products, not only do they consider the performance of the fund manager and the reputation of the fund company, but they are also concerned about the rate structure.

Types of fees of privately offered fund products

Investors have to pay different types of fees when they purchase a fund product. In this study, fees such as the front-end fee, administration fee (including custodian fee), and redemption fee are analyzed.

(1) Front-end fee: The amount paid by investors to purchase the fund during fundraising.

(2) Subscription fee: The amount paid by investors after fundraising during the duration of the fund.

(3) Redemption fee: During the duration of the funds, the amount paid by investors to withdraw from the fund.

(4) Administration fee: The fee collected by the fund management company or personnel.

(5) Custodian fee: The fee investors are charged by the custodian of the fund for safekeeping the fund assets and providing services.

(6) Others: Includes operational fee (attorneys' fees and CPA fees), liquidation fee, and taxes.

Features of the rates of sunshine private fund products

The features of the rates of sunshine private fund products are as follows:

The front-end fee is maintained at 1% without fluctuation.

The administration fee floats, but the majority of fees are over 1.5%. As shown in Table 7.3 and Table 7.4, the products with higher cumulative amounts charge a similar level of administration fee. The administration fee charged by privately offered fund companies of different size varies.

Redemption fee is charged based on the holding period. Redemption is usually not allowed during the lock-up period. After the lock-up period, the longer the holding period, the smaller the fee. Redemption usually does not incur charges after 12 months.

Comparison of the rates of privately offered fund products and public fund products

The major difference in rates between sunshine private funds and public funds is the charges. In general, sunshine private funds impose higher charges than public funds do, except for the front-end fee. This is because the product size of privately offered funds is smaller than that of public funds. They cannot capitalize on the economies of scale. It is also because of the small size so that they can lower the front-end fee to attract investors (See Table 7.5).

The rate structure of sunshine private fund companies is relatively mature and different from that of public fund companies.

Table 7.5   **Comparison of the rates of sunshine private fund products and public fund products**

	Sunshine private fund product	Public fund product
Minimum subscription amount	More; above RMB1 million	Less; usually above RMB1,000
Front-end fee	Usually 1%	Usually 1.2% or 1.5%
Administration fees	The sum of administration fee and custodian fee is usually equal to or larger than 1.5%.	Administration fee: Usually 1.5% for stock funds, lower than 1% for bond funds, and 0.33% for money market funds
		Custodian fee: Usually smaller than or equal to 0.25%
Redemption fee	More than 3%; no redemption fee after 12 months	Cannot exceed 3%; the longer the holding period, the lower the redemption fee

Source: Private Fund Research Center of Hua Ming Chuangfu Fund (HMC Fund).

Profit sharing in sunshine private fund products

Four types of sharing

The profits of public fund companies mainly come from administration fees. The profits of sunshine private fund companies mainly come from the allocation of returns on the products. Usually, the contract of trust products would include the clause that when the cumulative net value of the product is higher than the highest value on the historical open day, the trustee and investment consultant can obtain investment returns of the trust plan at a certain ratio based on the cumulative net value and the highest value. The sharing ratio is usually determined by four types of models. The examples below use a sample fund of RMB100 million. The actual sharing methods are based on the theoretical models below. A comparison between the net return of investors and the manager is made.

Fixed ratio

With a fixed ratio, regardless of the performance of the fund product, the fund company charges a fixed fee based on the net asset value of the fund product. This is the method adopted by public fund companies. This is their major source of profits. Fund managers are guaranteed stable income, but this method does not motivate fund managers.

For a RMB100 million stock public fund, the fixed ratio (administration fee) is usually 1.5%, which is to say the fund manager charges RMB1.5 million annually regardless of the rate of return on the product (See Fig. 7.15). The calculation is as follows:

RMB100,000,000 × 1.5% = RMB1,500,000

Fig. 7.15   Fixed sharing ratio

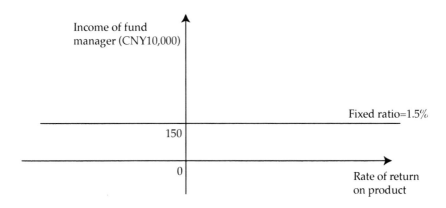

Source: Private Fund Research Center of Hua Ming Chuangfu Fund (HMC Fund).

Floating ratio

With a floating ratio, the fund company obtains a different proportion of profits based on the performance of the fund product. In China, the income of the fund company is usually calculated by multiplying the ratio with the annual profit. The higher the rate of return on the fund product, the higher the income of the fund company. If the fund product suffers a loss, the fund company cannot obtain income through profit sharing.

This method can increase the incentive of the fund managers as their income is based on the performance of the fund products. However, moral hazard is a great concern. The fund managers may pursue high-risk investments which may harm the interest of investors. At present, few companies adopt a single floating ratio. Most adopt a floating ratio with a minimum guarantee.

For example, a RMB1 million fund product obtains a 10% rate of return, and the floating ratio is 20%, the fund manager can obtain the following:

RMB100,000,000 × 10% × 20% = RMB2,000,000

Fig. 7.16   Floating sharing ratio

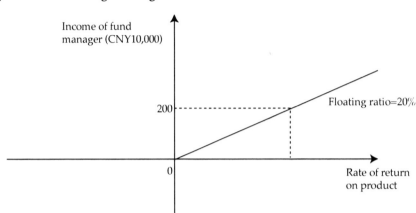

Source: Private Fund Research Center of Hua Ming Chuangfu Fund (HMC Fund).

Floating ratio with minimum guarantee

This is similar to and an improvement on the floating ratio method. In this method of floating ratio with minimum guarantee, the fund manager guarantees a fixed rate of return. Whether the product obtains a profit or suffers a loss, the fund manager would pay the investors their principal amount and a consented income. The investors are guaranteed to earn an income.

This method is more common in structured sunshine private fund products. The products are financed by the fund manager and investors at a certain ratio (usually 1:2). The parties on both sides agree on a yield to maturity. Then, the fund manager operates individually. When the product reaches maturity, regardless of the rate of return, the fund manager pays the investors at the rate agreed to in the contract. The remaining returns are allocated to the fund manager. By adopting this method, the investors are guaranteed a positive return, but the income of the fund manager is uncertain.

For a RMB100 million, structured, privately offered fund, if the fund is financed by the fund manager and investors at a ratio of 1:2, the former has to finance RMB33.33 million and the latter RMB66.67 million. Assume the agreed rate of return is 6%, the fund manager has to pay the investors RMB70.67 million including the principal amount and returns. It is calculated as follows:

RMB66,670,000 × （1+6%） = RMB70,670,200

When the rate of return on the product is 10%, the net income of the fund manager is calculated as follows:

RMB100,000,000 × 10% − RMBY66,670,000 × 6% = RMB5,999,800

The rate of return for the fund manager is as follows:

RMB5,999,800 ÷ RMB33,330,000 ≈ 18%

When the rate of return on the product is 4%, the rate of return for the fund manager is 0%. When the rate of return on the product is 0%, the rate of return for the fund manager is –12% (See Fig. 7.17).

Fig. 7.17   Floating sharing ratio with minimum guarantee

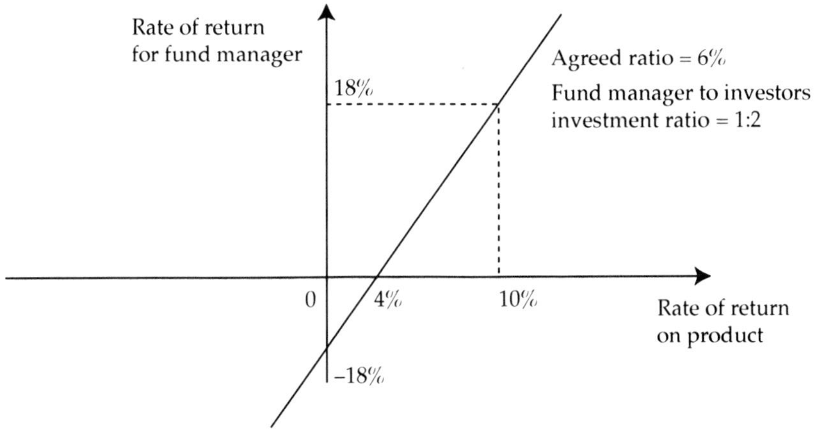

Source: Private Fund Research Center of Hua Ming Chuangfu Fund (HMC Fund).

Hybrid fixed and floating ratio

The hybrid method is a combination of both fixed ratio and floating ratio. The company charges a fixed administration fee and a floating investor fee. Among China's privately offered fund companies, some unstructured products of sunshine private fund companies adopt a similar profit sharing method. Unstructured products charge at a rate of 1.5% administration fee and 20% profit sharing ratio. The 1.5% of administration fee is a fixed ratio. The 20% sharing ratio is a floating ratio based on the rate of return on the product.

In RMB100 million unstructured privately offered funds, with a 1.5% fixed ratio, the fund manager charges a RMB1.5 million administration fee. When the rate of return on the product is equal to or smaller than 0%, the fund manager only receives a RMB1.5 million administration fee but no extra income. When the rate of return on the product is larger than 0%, the fund manager receives extra income based on the floating ratio. For example, with a 10% floating ratio, the income of the fund manager is RMB3.2 million as calculated below:

$$RMB100,000,000 \times 1.5\% + (RMB100,000,000 \times 10\% - RMB100,000,000 \times 1.5\%) \times 20\%$$
$$= RMB3,200,000$$

Fig. 7.18   Hybrid fixed and floating sharing ratio

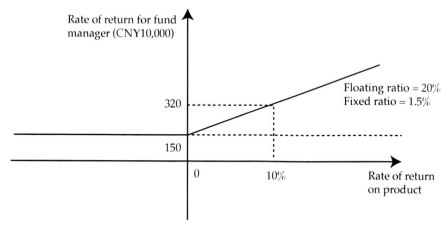

Source: Private Fund Research Center of Hua Ming Chuangfu Fund (HMC Fund).

Comparison of the net income of investors and the fund manager under the four types of profit sharing

Of the four methods of profit sharing, for investors, the floating rate with minimum guarantee brings the most stable net income. Regardless of the rate of return on the product, the investors gain RMB4 million given the size of the fund at RMB100 million. The net income in the other three methods changes with the rate of return on the product. While investors may obtain a huge amount of profit, they may also suffer a loss. To fund managers, the two methods which include a floating rate do not offer stability. If a product has a negative rate of return, the fund manager cannot receive any return or may receive negative returns. In the other two methods, the fund manager has a stable source of income from the fixed administration fee. In the hybrid method, the higher the rate of return on the product, the higher the net income for the fund manager. The comparison of the four methods is shown in Table 7.6.

Features of the profit sharing of sunshine private fund products

The products in Table 7.3 and Table 7.4 are unstructured products which all adopted the method of hybrid fixed and floating rates.[2] The floating rate at 20% has become an unspoken rule in the design of privately offered fund products. Of the information we collected, only Engine Investment's Jiutouniao 2 (sharing ratio at 19%), Zexi Investment Co., Ltd.'s Zexi Ruijin 1 (sharing ratio at 15%), Shenzhen Mingda Capital Management Co., Ltd.'s SZITIC Mingda 1 (sharing ratio at 22%) do not adopt the hybrid method.

In summary, sunshine private funds predominantly offer structured products with sharing methods of floating rates with minimum guarantee and unstructured products with hybrid fixed and floating rates.

Table 7.6   Comparison of the net income of investors and the fund manager under the four types of methods (RMB10,000)

| | | Rate of return on the product | | | | |
		−20%	10%	0%	10%	20%
Fixed ratio	Net income of investors	−2,150	−1,150	−150	850	1,850
	Net income of fund manager	150	150	150	150	150
Floating ratio	Net income of investors	−2,000	−1,000	0	800	1,600
	Net income of fund manager	0	0	0	200	400
Floating ratio with minimum guarantee	Net income of investors	400	400	400	400	400
	Net income of fund manager	−2,400	−1,400	−400	600	1,600
Hybrid fixed and floating ratios	Net income of investors	−2,150	−1,150	−150	680	1,480
	Net income of fund manager	150	150	−150	320	520

Note: Figures are rounded up to the unit digit.
Source: Private Fund Research Center of Hua Ming Chuangfu Fund (HMC Fund).

Prospect of China's Private Securities Investment Fund Companies

Private securities investment fund companies have been developing rapidly in recent years, especially sunshine private fund companies in terms of the number and size of products. However, sunshine private fund companies have encountered legal, sales, and human resources problems as they develop. The companies are in a bottleneck.

First, private securities investment funds are not granted legal status. This is the biggest obstacle to the development of the funds, especially to the sunshine private funds. Without legal status, sunshine private funds have to bear legal risk. In addition, they are suspended from opening trust accounts. Their cost for opening accounts is mounting.

Second, after years of development, sunshine private fund companies have developed their own structural organization, but there are problems with the structural balance. This is especially significant in the arrangement of the sales department. As the founder of sunshine privately offered fund companies usually supervise investment research. The companies usually focus on investment research and may neglect sales. As former public fund managers joined privately offered fund companies, more attention has been paid to the sales team and sales channels. The companies are more aware of the importance of the sales department. It is believed that the companies would pay equal attention to investment research and sales. The two departments would be developed simultaneously.

While the companies develop, they would be more concerned about internal risk control. In the past, due to the limited size of staff, the risk control department did not receive enough attention. However, the companies are aware of the importance of internal risk control for an investment institution. The risk-control department is gaining increasingly higher status in the companies.

Third, the team building and personnel training of the private securities investment fund companies are lagging behind the development of the companies themselves. This limits the development of the companies. The lack of talents and overly high human resources costs have caused several small sunshine private fund companies to be liquidated. This shows the importance of team building and personnel training. Only a development strategy centered on human resources can allow the companies to sustain development.

Fourth, as discussed in Chapter 6, the privately offered fund market is dominated by a few companies but there is fierce competition among products. This makes the companies more concerned about product innovation. Privately offered fund companies should launch personalized products with regard to the different needs of the investors and the character of the companies themselves. Division of labor, specialization, and product innovation would be the future trend of privately offered fund products.

Sunshine private fund companies have entered into a new stage after several years of development. They have encountered opportunities and challenges. The problems of some of the companies have started to surface. This triggered a reshuffling in the industry. Small and unregulated private securities investment fund companies are being eliminated. Large and regulated companies are gaining in size and market share thanks to the Matthew effect.

Furthermore, although sunshine private fund companies are the mainstream in the market of private securities investment funds, the share of sunshine private funds is still unsatisfactory. As the privately offered fund industry develops, the legal environment improves, investors become more educated, and there will be more sunshine private funds. As China's capital market opens up further, internationalization would become the new development trend among private securities investment fund companies. A number of the large sunshine private fund companies have expanded overseas. In the future, private securities investment fund companies would develop in the overseas market and transform into sunshine private fund companies.

Appendix

Table 7.7   Top 100 sunshine private fund companies by the number of products as of May 31, 2011

Rank	Sunshine private fund company	Central figure	Number of products	Date of launch
1	Shanghai Elegant Investment Co., Ltd.	Shi Bo	36	August 31, 2007
2	Rosefinch Investment Co., Ltd.	Li Hualun	33	July 2, 2007
3	Beijing StarRock Investment Management Co., Ltd.	Jiang Hui	28	June 28, 2007
4	Springs Capital (Beijing) Ltd.	Zhao Jun	27	June 2007
5	Shanghai Congrong Investment Management Co., Ltd.	Lü Jun	26	November 30, 2007
6	Shenzhen Wudang Asset Management Ltd.	Tian Ronghua	22	June 30, 2007
7	Bohong (Tianjin) Fund Management Co., Ltd.	Liu Hong	20	August 2003
8	Shanghai Huili Asset Management Co., Ltd.	He Zhen	19	March 31, 2008
9	Shanghai Vstone Investment Consulting Co., Ltd.	Chen Jiwu	19	October 9, 2008
10	Guangdong New Value Investment Co., Ltd.	Li Tao	18	August 31, 2007
11	Shenzhen Hanxin Asset Management Co., Ltd.	Jiang Guoyun	17	January 18, 2010
12	Beijing Longrising Asset Management Co., Ltd.	Zeng Xiaojie	12	March 31, 2008
13	Shenzhen Minsen Investment Co., Ltd.	Cai Ming	12	March 31, 2007
14	Shenzhen Sinowise Investment Co., Ltd.	—	12	February 2009

Table 7.7   Top 100 sunshine private fund companies by the number of products as of May 31, 2011

(Cont'd)

Rank	Sunshine private fund company	Central figure	Number of products	Date of launch
15	Shanghai Wisdom Investment Managers Co., Ltd.	Wu Jun	12	April 30, 2008
16	Yuance Investment Management Co., Ltd.	Zhang Yici	11	August 31, 2009
17	Shanghai Chongyang Investment Management Co., Ltd.	Qiu Guogen	11	December 31, 2001
18	Guangzhou Long-Term Investment Asset Management Co., Ltd.	Zheng Xiaojun	11	November 30, 2007
19	Shanghai Dingfeng Asset Management Corporation	Zhang Gao	11	December 31, 2007
20	Shenzhen Kangcheng Heng Investment Co., Ltd.	Yuan Yakang	10	December 31, 2007
21	Shenzhen Golden Investment Management Co., Ltd.	Zeng Jun	10	February 28, 2007
22	Shanghai Chaos Investment Co., Ltd.	Ge Weidong	10	—
23	Sycomore Private Asset Management Co., Ltd.	Yang Lianqi	10	September 24, 2008
24	Liuhe Capital, LLC.	Xia Xiaohui	9	August 25, 2004
25	Shanghai Milestone Asset Management Co., Ltd.	Cheng Yiquan	9	May 31, 2007
26	TeamTop Investment Co., Ltd.	Cheng Nenghong	9	April 30, 2007
27	Co-Power Capital Management Co., Ltd.	Li Ci	9	December 31, 2008
28	Beijing Heju Investment Management Co., Ltd.	Li Zegang	8	March 27, 2009
29	Hangzhou Huian Investment Co, Ltd.	Shen Yihui	8	November 20, 2008
30	Yrd Investment (Beijing) Co., Ltd.	Cao Xiangjun	8	April 30, 2006
31	Shanghai Yiju Investment Co, Ltd.	Liu Huainan	8	July 31, 2001
32	Shanghai Zhengda Investment Management Co., Ltd.	Zhu Nansong	7	April 21, 1994
33	Shenzhen Gemboom Investment Co., Ltd.	Chen Feng	7	—
34	Rising Investment Management Co., Ltd.	Li Zhenning	7	December 10, 2007
35	Greenwoods Asset Management Ltd.	Jiang Jinzhi	7	January 1, 2004

Table 7.7   **Top 100 sunshine private fund companies by the number of products as of May 31, 2011**

(Cont'd)

Rank	Sunshine private fund company	Central figure	Number of products	Date of launch
36	Beijing Eastern Vision Asset Management Co., Ltd.	Xu Yong	6	September 30, 2007
37	Shenzhen Heying Investment Management Co., Ltd.	Zeng Zhaoxiong	6	March 31, 2007
38	Ivy Asset Management Co., Ltd.	—	6	November 30, 2010
39	Jiangsu Winlast Investment Holding Group Co., Ltd.	—	6	July 2, 2003
40	Munsun Asset Management Ltd.	Chen Baodong	6	—
41	Guangdong RuiTian Investment Management Co., Ltd.	Li Peng	6	Septem 10, 2007
42	World Versed Asset Management Co., Ltd.	Chang Shishan	6	—
43	Shenzhen Growing Wealth Investment Co., Ltd.	Tang Xuelai	6	—
44	Guangdong Xiyu Investment & Management Co., Ltd.	Zhou Shuijiang	6	July 31, 2007
45	Shanghai Honghu Investment Management Ltd.	Liang Wentao	6	December 31, 2010
46	Hubei Engine Investment Co., Ltd.	Li Shaowei	5	—
47	Beijing Jingfu Rongyuan Investment Management Co., Ltd.	Li Yanwei	5	December 23, 2007
48	Gloria Investments Management Co., Ltd.	Wang Guiwen	5	July 31, 2007
49	Capital Fortune Asset Management Ltd.	Chen Shan	5	August 31, 2007
50	Shanghai Sunsource Investment & Development Co., Ltd.	Li Wei	5	—
51	Batach-Sophia Investment Management Co., Ltd.	Leng Guobang	5	August 31, 2007
52	Goldstone Investment Ltd.	Yao Hongbin	5	December 31, 2007
53	Shanghai Vanfon Youfang Investing Co., Ltd.	—	5	December 31, 2004
54	Shanghai Spring Capital Co., Ltd.	—	5	—
55	Beijing Sun Capital Investment Management Co., Ltd.	Sun Jiandong	5	March 31, 2010

Table 7.7   Top 100 sunshine private fund companies by the number of products as of May 31, 2011

(Cont'd)

Rank	Sunshine private fund company	Central figure	Number of products	Date of launch
56	Shenzhen Longteng Assets Management Co., Ltd.	Wu Xianfeng	5	February 26, 2007
57	Shanghai Zexi Investment Management Co., Ltd.	Xu Xiang	5	December 7, 2009
58	Fangde Asset Management Co., Ltd.	Zhou Xinchang	5	March 31, 2007
59	YCT Investment Management Co., Ltd.	—	4	August 1, 2006
60	Shenzhen Mingda Capital Management Co., Ltd.	Liu Mingda	4	December 31, 2005
61	New Top-Founder Investment Management Co., Ltd.	Liu Xun	4	December 24, 1997
62	Shanghai G-Share Investment Management Co., Ltd.	Xia Ning	4	December 31, 2007
63	Shanghai Guanjun Asset Management Co., Ltd.	—	4	—
64	Shanghai Rongwei Investment Co., Ltd.	—	4	August 26, 2003
65	King Tower Asset Management Co., Ltd.	Zhang Yingbiao	4	March 29, 2007
66	Shenzhen Zhonglu Wealth Ltd.	Xue Feng	4	December 31, 1999
67	Shenzhen Ming Yuan Investment Co., Ltd.	Lu Wei	4	—
68	Shanghai Broadvision Investment Management Co., Ltd.	Xu Dacheng	4	December 31, 2007
69	Longwin Asset Management Co., Ltd.	Tong Diyi	4	December 31, 2006
70	Shenzhen Megastar Investment Management Co., Ltd.	—	4	—
71	Shanghai Xinfangchen Investment Management Co., Ltd.	—	4	December 31, 2007
72	Shanghai Beita Investment Management Co., Ltd.	Xu Hongjuan	4	December 31, 2006
73	Shanghai Simple Asset Management, L.P.	Yang Dian	4	June 30, 2009
74	Shanghai Chengrui Assets Management Co., Ltd.	Rui Kun	4	May 31, 2010
75	Zhejiang Linyi Investment & Management Corporation	Chen Hao	4	—

Table 7.7 **Top 100 sunshine private fund companies by the number of products as of May 31, 2011**

(Cont'd)

Rank	Sunshine private fund company	Central figure	Number of products	Date of launch
76	Shenzhen Pole Point Assets Management Co., Ltd.	Chen Wentao	4	November 30, 2007
77	Guangzhou Anzhou Investment Management Co., Ltd.	—	3	April 30, 2005
78	Kingfortune Asset Management Co., Ltd.	Wang Jin	3	March 31, 2006
79	Shanghai Tajing Investment Management Co., Ltd.	Leng Zaiqing	3	—
80	Shanghai Lühe Investment Co., Ltd.	—	3	—
81	Shenzheng City Boien Investment LLC	Long Xiaobo	3	May 31, 2004
82	Sunshine & Fortuneguard Asset Management Co., Ltd.	Liu Ying	3	November 30, 2010
83	Prime Capital Management Co., Ltd.	Liu Hongmei	3	December 31, 1997
84	Yitian Investment Management Co., Ltd.	Ye Fei	3	December 31, 2010
85	Shanghai Daoheng Asset Management Co., Ltd.	—	3	—
86	Zhejiang Xinxinkairui Investment Management Co., Ltd.	—	3	—
87	YJA Investments	Jin Yi	3	—
88	Beijing Xinyuan Lanzhong Investment Management Co., Ltd.	Wang Shuai	3	December 31, 2009
89	Shanghai Sunny Investment Management Co.,Ltd.	Sun Zhihong	3	—
90	Gainful Investment Corp.	Chen Haifeng	3	April 30, 2007
91	Shanghai Jingyi Investment Manage Co., Ltd.	—	3	December 31, 2002
92	Zhongzi Eastern Capital Management Co., Ltd.	—	3	March 31, 2009
93	Shenzhen Linyuan Investment Ltd	Lin Yuna	3	March 23, 2004
94	James & Hina Capital Management Co., Ltd.	Wang Weidong	3	March 31, 2007
95	Shenzhen Elitimes Investment & Management Co., Ltd.	Cheng Hongchao	3	—

Table 7.7   Top 100 sunshine private fund companies by the number of
products as of May 31, 2011

(Cont'd)

Rank	Sunshine private fund company	Central figure	Number of products	Date of launch
96	Shenzhen Lighthorse Asset Management Co., Ltd.	Kang Xiaoyang	3	January 17, 2002
97	Shenzhen Lisheng Ruihua Investment Co., Ltd.	Huang Guohai	3	September 30, 2009
98	Shanghai Qianshi Investment Management Co., Ltd.	—	3	May 7, 2010
99	Shanghai PurpleStone Investment Ltd.	Zhang Chao	3	April 30, 2007
100	Beijing Sensegain Investment Management Co., Ltd.	Zhang Liqun	3	August 31, 2006

Note: The table is presented with public data. A number of funds did not release information. Inaccuracies are minimized.

Source: Data from Wind Info analyzed by the Private Fund Research Center of Hua Ming Chuangfu Fund (HMC Fund).

8

Chapter

Analysis of Private Non-Securities Investment Funds

Private equity funds, as an important type of investment funds, is a major financing channel in the primary market. China's private equity investment began in 1986. After more than 20 years of development, the private equity industry has grown to a considerable size.

Private equity funds and private securities investment funds differ in a lot of aspects. Different from private securities investment funds, China's private equity funds developed with government support. The government utilizes private equity investment as a channel to guide investment and attract foreign investment. Real private equity funds offered by the private sector are limited. Investment companies with a foreign or government background have strong financial power. They are the major force in China's private equity market.

Private equity funds may refer to traditional private equity (PE) funds and venture capital (VC) funds.[1] The size of private real estate investment funds is limited. However, in the past two years, their development has been rapid. It is possible that they would become a major source of investment in the privately offered fund industry in the near future.

This chapter presents the history, features, and current situation of private non-securities investment funds, including PE funds, VC funds, and private real estate investment funds.

Development Situation of Private Equity Funds

Information on the private equity market is not transparent. Based on the data revealed by investment companies, we present an overview of the fundraising, investment, withdrawal, and returns of private equity funds.

Fundraising

During 2006 to 2008, with the effect of government encouragement and market development, both PE and VC funds rapidly developed in terms of the number and size of funds. The development hit its climax in 2008. In 2009, due to the influence of the financial crisis, the amount of funds raised dropped dramatically. The fundraising of VC funds picked up in the following year and hit a record high of USD11.17 billion. The year-on-year growth was 90.7%. The number of funds also grew to 158, a 68.1% year-on-year growth. In 2010, the number of and amount of funds raised by PE funds also reached 82 and USD27.62 billion, a 173.3% and 113.2% year-on-year growth, respectively. The scale was, however, not comparable to before the financial crisis (See Fig. 8.1). In the first half of 2011, the total amount of funds raised by both VC and PE had exceeded half the amount in 2010. There was a growing trend. Compared to VC funds, PE funds raise a greater amount of funds and the size of a single fund was larger.

Fig. 8.1 **Fundraising of VC and PE funds during 2006 to the first half of 2011**

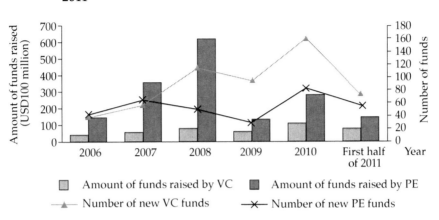

Source: Data from the Zero2IPO Research Center analyzed by the Private Fund Research Center of Hua Ming Chuangfu Fund (HMC Fund).

Since 2006, the amount of renminbi raised by VC funds has continued to increase. In 2009, the amount surpassed the amount raised by foreign VC funds. In that year, the number of and amount of funds raised by foreign VC funds decreased significantly but recovered rapidly in 2010. The growth rate in the amount of funds was close to 100%. In the first half of 2011, the amount of renminbi and foreign currency raised continued to grow (See Fig. 8.2). Foreign funds maintained the advantage of having a larger size for a single fund in comparison to renminbi funds.

Fig. 8.2 **VC fundraising sources during 2006 to the first half of 2011**

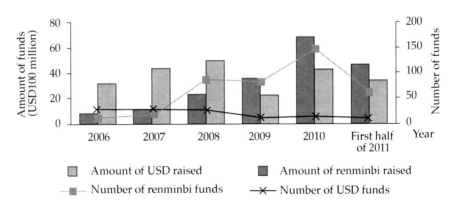

Source: Data from the Zero2IPO Research Center analyzed by the Private Fund Research Center of Hua Ming Chuangfu Fund (HMC Fund).

During 2006 to 2010, both renminbi and foreign investment funds were developing. Apart from being under the effect of the financial crisis in 2009, foreign PE funds dominated (See Fig. 8.3). According to the data of the first half of 2011, the development momentum of renminbi private funds was strong. The total amount of funds raised was expected to grow higher. The momentum of foreign PE funds weakened despite the size of a single foreign PE fund which remained higher.

Fig. 8.3   **PE fundraising sources during 2006 to the first half of 2011**

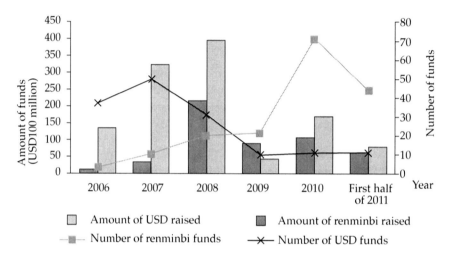

Source: Data from the Zero2IPO Research Center analyzed by the Private Fund Research Center of Hua Ming Chuangfu Fund (HMC Fund).

Investment

During 2006 to 2010, the number and amount of investment of VC funds grew steadily except for the significant drop in 2009. In 2010, number and amount of investment hit a record high with growth rates of 71.3% and 99.4%. In the first half of 2011, the total investment of VC had exceeded the total investment in the entire year of 2010.

During 2006 to 2010, the number and amount of investment of PE funds were on a continuous fall. The number and amount of investment bounced back in 2010 with a growth rate of 210.3% and 20%, respectively. In the first half of 2011, the growth in PE investment was huge. The amount was close to the total investment in the entire year of 2010. The amount of a single investment also recovered. The PE market was highly active in 2011. The average amount of funds per investment remained higher than that of VC funds (See Fig. 8.4).

Fig. 8.4   VC and PE investment during 2006 to the first half of 2011

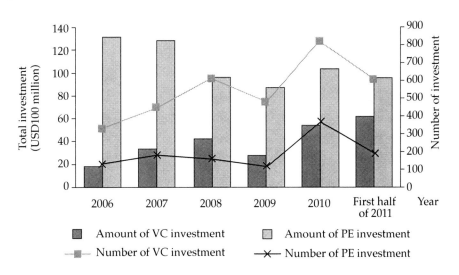

Source: Data from the Zero2IPO Research Center analyzed by the Private Fund Research
Center of Hua Ming Chuangfu Fund (HMC Fund).

As shown in Table 8.1, the percentage share of investment in of renminbi and foreign currencies was similar in VC and PE funds in 2010. In terms of the number of investments, renminbi had a greater share than foreign currencies. However, the amount of funds per investment in renminbi was also smaller than that in foreign currencies.

Table 8.1   Percentage share of investment in of renminbi and foreign currencies in VC and PE funds in 2010

	Number of investments in VC	Percentage share (%)	Amount of investments in VC	Percentage share (%)	Number of investments in PE	Percentage share (%)	Amount of investments in PE	Percentage share (%)
Renminbi	525	64	27.77	52	239	65	56.91	55
Foreign currencies	245	30	26.10	48	111	31	46.90	45
Unknown	47	6	—	—	13	4	—	—

Source: Data from the Zero2IPO Research Center analyzed by the Private Fund Research
Center of Hua Ming Chuangfu Fund (HMC Fund).

Looking at the investment by industry, the number and amount of VC investments was the highest in the internet industry. Other leading industries were clean technology, biotechnology/healthcare, machinery manufacturing, and information technology (See Fig. 8.5). The situation was similar in the first half of 2011. The number and amount of VC investments in the internet industry reached 110 and USD1.55 billion.

Fig. 8.5   Distribution of VC investments by industry in 2010

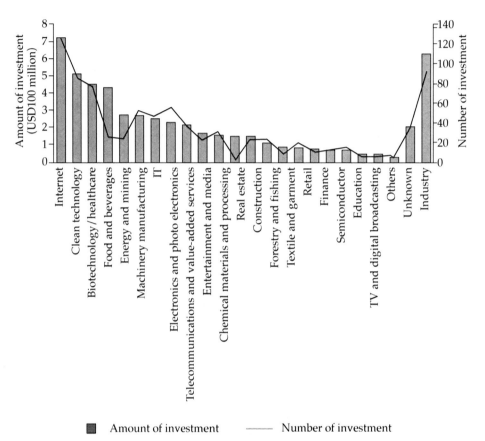

Source: Data from the Zero2IPO Research Center analyzed by the Private Fund Research Center of Hua Ming Chuangfu Fund (HMC Fund).

In the distribution of PE investment by industry in 2010, biotechnology/healthcare topped the list in terms of the number of investments, and machinery manufacturing in terms of the amount of investment. Other popular industries were internet, retail, forestry and fishing, and food and beverages (See Fig. 8.6). In the first half of 2011, the increase in PE investment in biotechnology/healthcare was huge. The number and amount of investment rose to 22 and USD3.11 billion, ranked first among all industries. The increase in investment in the internet industry also picked up. The number and amount of investments grew to 21 and USD1.13 billion.

Fig. 8.6 Distribution of PE investments by industry in 2010

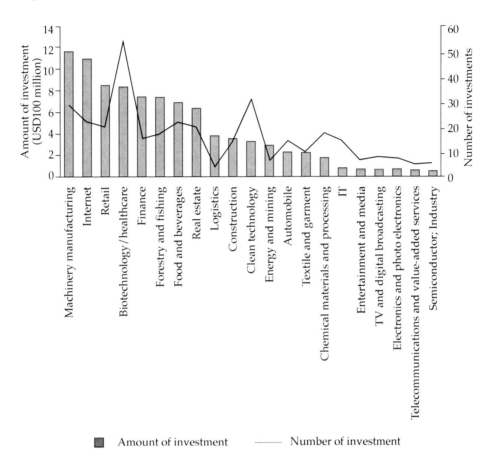

Amount of investment   -------- Number of investment

Source: Data from the Zero2IPO Research Center analyzed by the Private Fund Research
Center of Hua Ming Chuangfu Fund (HMC Fund).

The distribution of investments by region in 2010 was similar for both VC and PE investments. Beijing was the location with the most number and amount of investments. Shanghai, Jiangsu Province, Zhejiang Province, and Guangdong Province (excluding Shenzhen) were other regions with greater investment activity (See Fig. 8.7 and Fig. 8.8). In the first half of 2011, Kohlberg Kravis Roberts & Co. L.P. acquired CAPSUGEL. This contributed to the USD2.67 billion investments in Jiangsu Province. VC and PE investments concentrated in the southeast coastal areas and developed regions thanks to the local preferential policies.

Fig. 8.7   Distribution of VC investments by region in 2010

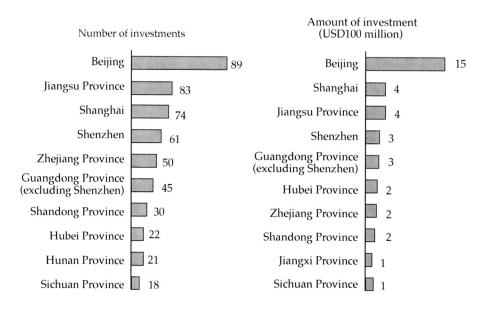

Source: Data from the Zero2IPO Research Center analyzed by the Private Fund Research
Center of Hua Ming Chuangfu Fund (HMC Fund).

Fig. 8.8   Distribution of PE investments by region in 2010

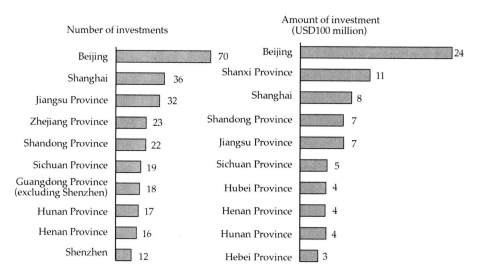

Source: Data from the Zero2IPO Research Center analyzed by the Private Fund Research
Center of Hua Ming Chuangfu Fund (HMC Fund).

Withdrawal

The number of China's IPO companies with a VC or PE background grew 185.7% in 2010 compared to 2009. The amount of funds raised through IPO hit a record high of USD37.37 billion, a 174.2% growth from the previous year (See Fig. 8.9). Such significant growth was a result of the launch of the growth enterprise market (GEM) in China, which acted as a major platform for the withdrawal of private equity funds.

Fig. 8.9   IPO of companies with a VC or PE background in China in 2010

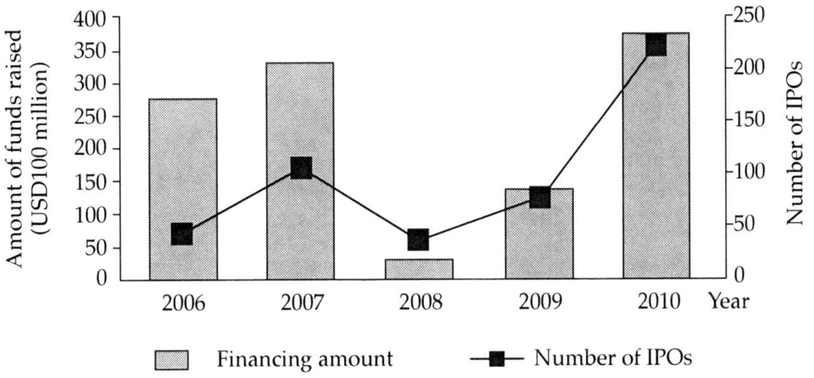

Source: ChinaVenture, http://www.chinaventure.com.cn.

In the first half of 2011, 71 VC companies and 45 PE companies became listed, accounting for 198 and 61 cases of withdrawal, respectively.[2]

In 2010, machinery manufacturing was the industry with the most VC withdrawal. Other industries with a considerable number of withdrawals were information technology, internet, clean technology, electronics and photo electronics, telecommunications and value-added services, and biotechnology/healthcare (See Fig. 8.10)

In 2010, machinery manufacturing was also the industry with the most PE withdrawals, followed by biotechnology/healthcare, and food and beverages (Fig. 8.11).

In 2010, the major method of withdrawal was IPO, which accounted for 85.31% of VC withdrawals and 96% of PE withdrawals (See Fig. 8.12 and Fig. 8.13).

In the first quarter of 2011, the percentage of withdrawals through IPO rose to 86.8% for VC and 98% for PE. Other withdrawal methods included mergers and acquisitions, equity transfer, and repurchase.

Fig. 8.10 VC withdrawals by industry in 2010

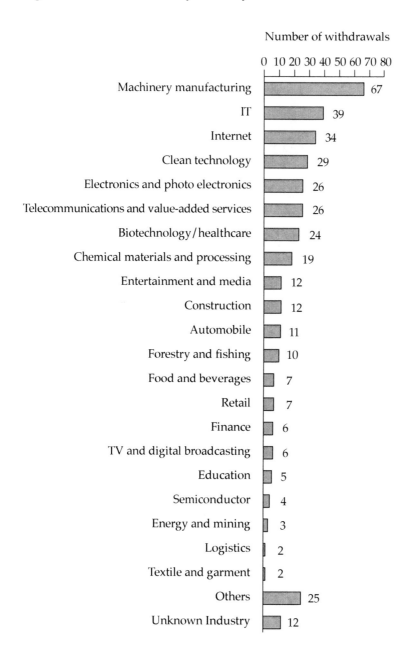

Source: Data from the Zero2IPO Research Center analyzed by the Private Fund Research Center of Hua Ming Chuangfu Fund (HMC Fund).

Fig. 8.11 PE withdrawal by industry in 2010

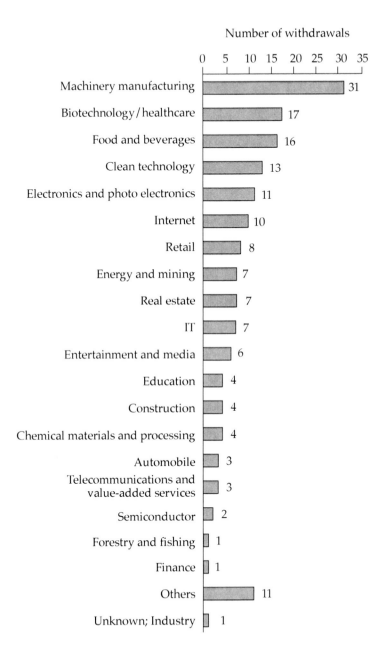

Source: Data from the Zero2IPO Research Center analyzed by the Private Fund Research Center of Hua Ming Chuangfu Fund (HMC Fund).

Fig. 8.12   Percentage share of VC withdrawal methods in 2010

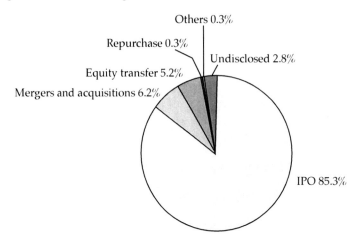

Source: Data from the Zero2IPO Research Center analyzed by the Private Fund Research
Center of Hua Ming Chuangfu Fund (HMC Fund).

Fig. 8.13   Percentage share of PE withdrawal methods in 2010

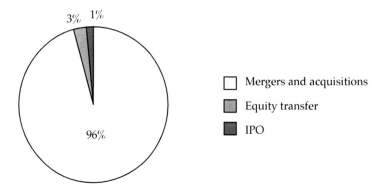

Source: Data from the Zero2IPO Research Center analyzed by the Private Fund Research
Center of Hua Ming Chuangfu Fund (HMC Fund).

The IPO withdrawals of VC companies concentrate in the GEM and small and medium-sized enterprise (SME) board market in the Shenzhen Stock Exchange (SZSE). The IPO withdrawals of VC companies is mainly through the main board market in the Hong Kong Stock Exchange (SEHK), together with the New York Stock Exchange (NYSE), the GEM and small and medium-sized enterprise board market in the Shenzhen Stock Exchange (See Fig. 8.14). The difference in investment styles of VC and PE funds led to the difference in withdrawal channels.

Fig. 8.14   Analysis of VC and PE withdrawal in 2010

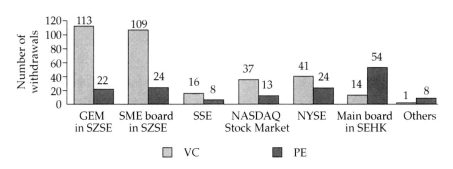

Source: Data from the Zero2IPO Research Center analyzed by the Private Fund Research
          Center of Hua Ming Chuangfu Fund (HMC Fund).

As the GEM and SME board were launched in the SZSE, they quickly became the major board markets for VC and PE withdrawal. VC and PE funds no longer rely on mergers and acquisitions and repurchases for withdrawals like they used to.

Returns

The information on the private equity market is not transparent. The study of the returns on VC and PE here is based on the rate of return on the IPO of the funds. From 2006 to 2010, the return on private equity funds was high after they became listed through IPO. The return was 11.23 times in 2009 and 8.06 times in 2010. The return of some of the funds was as high as 540 times (See Fig. 8.15).

Fig. 8.15   Average rates of return on the IPO of VC and PE funds during 2006–2010

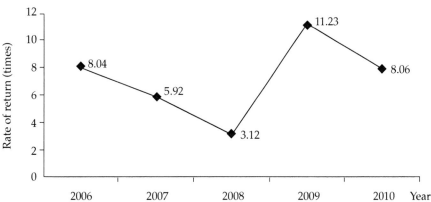

Source: ChinaVenture, http://www.chinaventure.com.cn.

Development Situation of Private Equity Fund Companies

After more than 20 years of development, there are currently 379 private equity companies in China's market.[3] As the fund manager of private equity funds, the behavior of the company directly influences the development of the industry. According to the Zero2IPO Research Center's *2010 China Venture Capital & Private Equity Annual Ranking*, the top 50 VC and top 30 PE funds were chosen as subjects in this study. There were 79 representative private equity fund companies.[4] The features of the organization, human resources, and products of the private equity fund companies are discussed below.

Features of organization

Legal form

A private equity company can be formed as a corporate type or limited partnership company. At present, the majority of companies adopt the form of a limited company. Limited partnership became a legal form of private equity companies after the announcement of the 2007 *Partnership Enterprise Law*. Few private equity companies adopt the form of a limited partnership. Of the 79 companies in this study, Boxin Capital was the only limited partnership private equity investment company.

Nature of capital

The sources of capital of private equity investment companies are complex. In this study, the companies are classified by their sources of capital into state-owned, foreign, and others.

The representatives of state-owned companies are Shenzhen Capital Group Co., Ltd., and Hunan Xiangtou High-Tech Venture Capital Co., Ltd. Those of foreign companies include IDG Capital Partners and Softbank China Venture Capital Ltd. The sources of capital of other companies are diverse. The sources can be a combination of state-owned and foreign capital, state-owned and private capital, private and foreign capital, or large private investment institutions. The classification of the 79 private equity companies is shown in Fig. 8.16.

Fig. 8.16   Classification of the 79 private equity companies

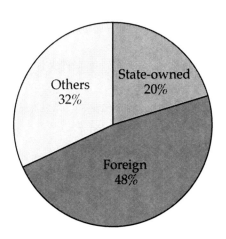

Source: Data from the EZCapital, CYZone, and company websites analyzed by the Private
          Fund Research Center of Hua Ming Chuangfu Fund (HMC Fund).

From early on, the government supported the development of private equity investment with an aim to guide investment and introduce foreign capital. It is not surprising that the majority of private equity investment companies are state-owned or foreign-owned. Such companies assume unparalleled advantages. In contrast, the number of other private equity investment companies, especially those established with private capital, remains small despite two years of rapid development. Their financial strength is weak compared to the state-owned and foreign companies. The situation is different from that of private securities investment companies.

Location of headquarters

The top five locations with the most headquarters of China's private equity investment companies are Beijing, Shanghai, the U.S., Shenzhen, and Hong Kong (See Fig.8.17).

The headquarters of foreign private equity companies are usually overseas although many of them set up a China headquarters in Beijing, Shanghai, or Shenzhen. The headquarters of state-owned private equity companies are located mainly in Beijing, Shanghai, Shenzhen, and Hong Kong. Some are located in the capital cities of provinces.

Fig. 8.17   Locations of the headquarters of China's private equity investment companies

Wuhan 1%

Suzhou 1%   Nanjing 1%

Changsha 1%   Singapore 1%

Hangzhou 4%

Hong Kong 10%   Beijing 32%

Shenzhen 13%

Shanghai 19%

U.S. 17%

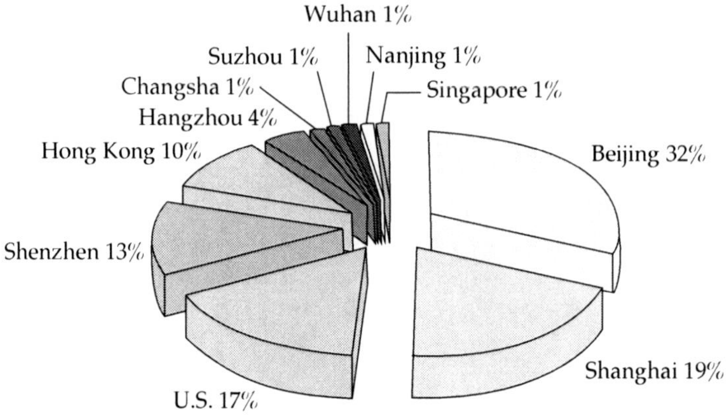

Source: Data from the EZCapital, CYZone, and company websites analyzed by the Private Fund Research Center of Hua Ming Chuangfu Fund (HMC Fund).

Features of human resources

Number of employees

Different from private securities investment companies, the research team of the private equity investment companies is large. A large company employs than 100 researchers. Even smaller companies have a team of more than 20 researchers.

Quality of employees

Private equity investment companies need investment professionals to make investment decisions for the companies. They need researchers with multidisciplinary education and professional experience.

A lot of foreign private equity investment companies employ researchers with overseas education or working experience. China's private equity investment companies also employ a lot of researchers who have been educated overseas.

Features of products

Legal form

Similar to other privately offered funds, there are three legal forms of private equity funds: contract type, corporate type, and limited partnership. With government support and encouragement, there is no suspension on the opening of any investment accounts. There are more private equity investment companies in the form of limited partnerships compared to private securities investment companies.

Compared to other legal forms, limited partnership assumes advantages in taxation, profit sharing, incentive mechanism, and the rights of equity. This paves the way for better development. The development of China's limited partnership private equity investment companies was relatively late. The companies did not gain legal status until the *Partnership Enterprise Law* was announced. On June 28, 2007, the first limited partnership private equity fund in China — Shenzhen Southern Ocean Development Featured Venture Capital Partnership LLP — was established by Shenzhen Cowin Venture Capital Investments Ltd. This signified the beginning of marketized operation of private equity funds through limited partnership.

Currently, the number of corporate type and limited partnership private equity investment companies is more or less equal.

Investment

Each private equity investment company has its own stages of investment. The stage of investment usually determines the stage of the products (See Fig. 8.18).

Fig. 8.18   Investment stages of private equity investment companies

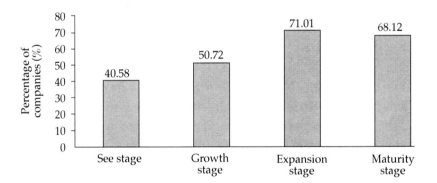

Sources: Data from the EZCapital, CYZone, and company websites analyzed by the Private
Fund Research Center of Hua Ming Chuangfu Fund (HMC Fund).

At present, the distribution of companies spreads over a wide range of investment stages. 70.01% of companies are in the expansion stage and 40.58% are in the seed stage.

Overview of China's Private Real Estate Investment Funds

Real estate is the new direction of investment of China's private equity funds. Compared to other countries, China's private real estate investment funds are still in the initial development stage.

There are multiple ways to classify private real estate investment funds. The funds are usually classified into trust funds launched by trust companies and private equity real estate funds launched by PE management companies. The research and statistics system of China's private real estate investment funds is inadequate.

Trust type private real estate investment funds

Trust type private real estate investment funds are developed under the framework of the *Trust Law*. They are issued by trust companies as contract type funds.

Since the announcement of the *Notice on Further Strengthening the Administration of Real Estate Credit* in 2003, trust type private real estate investment funds hit a record high in the amount of funds raised at RMB15.73 billion in two years' time. In 2005, the China Banking Regulatory Commission (CBRC) issued the *Notice on Strengthening Risk Disclosure of Partial Business of Trust Investment Companies (No. 212)*. In August 2006, the CBRC issued the *Notice on Further Strengthening the Administration of Real Estate Credit* again and demanded a strict execution of regulations stated in the *Notice on Strengthening Risk Disclosure of Partial Business of Trust Investment Companies (No. 212)*. In 2006 and 2007, trust type private real estate investment funds entered into a period of adjustment. The amount of funds raised was limited. In 2008, under the effect of the macroeconomic regulation and control, the regulation of the financing channels of the real estate industry was rigorous. Trust type private real estate investment funds were considered by real estate enterprises again. The amount of funds raised climbed quickly. Especially in 2010 when the real estate industry was under very rigorous macroeconomic regulation and control, the equity financing channels of the real estate enterprises were cut off. This presented opportunities for trust type private real estate investment funds to develop. They raised RMB192.1 billion funds. In the first four months of 2011, they have raised RMB72.21 billion. The funds are on a period of recovery and accelerated growth (See Fig. 8.19).

Fig. 8.19   Amount of funds raised by trust type private real estate investment funds, 2003–2011

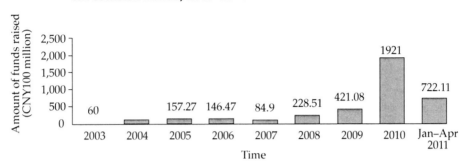

Sources: Data from the Southwestern University of Finance and Economics Research Institute of Trusts and Finance, CNBenefit, Real Estate Finance Industry Risk Analysis Reports, and Use Trust Studio analyzed by the Private Fund Research Center of Hua Ming Chuangfu Fund (HMC Fund).

According to Hexun (Hexun.com), the lock-up period of the 359 products in 2010 and 10 products in 2011 ranged from six months to 60 months with a prevalence of 24 months. The average issue size of products in 2010 was RMB326 million and that of products in 2011 was RMB429 million. The investment threshold for trust type real estate investment funds is usually RMB1 million with a few products having a lower threshold at RMB500,000 and even RMB100,000.

Fig. 8.20 shows the types of investment of trust type real estate investment funds issued in 2010. Trust loans and equity investments were the major types of investment. The number of investment of both types was similar. Investment in equity rights was the third most popular type.

Fig. 8.20   Types of investment of trust type real estate investment funds in 2010

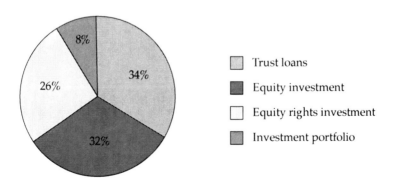

Source: Data from the Hexun.com analyzed by the Private Fund Research Center of Hua Ming Chuangfu Fund (HMC Fund).

The average rate of return on trust type private real estate investment fund projects was 8.4% in 2010. It rose to 12.56% in 2011 thanks to the stricter regulation over the financing channels and higher financing cost of the industry.

Private equity real estate investment funds

Private equity real estate investment funds are established under the framework of private equity funds. They invest in real estate and are managed by fund management companies. At present, the majority of private equity real estate investment funds exist as limited partnerships. Some exist as corporate type funds. There are very few contract type funds.

The development of private equity real estate investment funds is similar to that of private equity funds. Both are driven by foreign capital. As early as in the 1990s, leading foreign investment institutions such as ING and Goldman Sachs began to launch real estate investment funds with a focus on China's market. Up to 2009, foreign capital had been dominating China's private equity real estate investment market. As financing became more difficult and the cost of financing continued to rise in China, China's domestic private equity real estate investment funds developed rapidly after 2009. In 2010, 10 of China's private equity real estate investment funds raised a total of USD1.86 billion. In the first half of 2011, seven funds raised a total of USD1.13 billion. The amount was expected to climb in the second half of the year. In 2010, 90% of the number of funds and 80% of the amount of funds were domestic funds and capital in China. There were four domestic funds in the first half of 2011. They raised a total of USD417 million.[5]

According to the statistics of Richlink International Capital Co., Ltd., as of the end of 2010, there were 47 private equity real estate funds in the China market. 58% were foreign funds and 38% were domestic funds (See Fig. 8.21). 83% were limited partnership funds and only one was a contract type fund (See Fig. 8.22).

Fig. 8.21   Sources of capital of private equity real estate investment funds

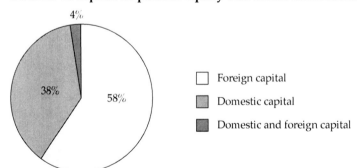

Source: Richlink International Capital Co., Ltd., *2010 China's Real Estate Finance Report*, http://www.richlink.com.cn/RichlinkResearch1.htm.

Fig. 8.22 **Legal forms of capital of private equity real estate investment funds**

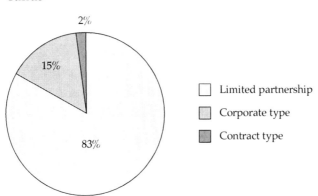

Source: Richlink International Capital Co., Ltd., *2010 China's Real Estate Finance Report*, http://www.richlink.com.cn/RichlinkResearch1.htm.

Evaluation and Prospects of the Development of China's Private Equity Funds

With constant improvements in the external environment, the private equity market enters into a stage of rational development

As China's economy develops, the capital in the market looks for investment channels. Since 2005, the government has implemented a variety of policies and regulations to stimulate the growth of private equity funds. Intellectual property rights are getting more attention and this attention will facilitate the development of scientific and technological innovation-oriented enterprises. Moreover, the developing multi-layered capital market offers a better withdrawal channel for private equity funds. This helps motivate the development of private equity funds.

Simultaneous development of domestic and foreign private equity fund companies

In the past 10 years, the steady and rapid growth of private equity funds has surpassed foreign private equity funds in terms of the number of funds and total amount of funds. However, the average amount of funds raised and the investment scale are still lagging behind foreign private equity funds. The competition in the industry is keen.

Foreign private equity funds were first developed in the 1940s and entered China in the 1990s. Foreign private equity investment companies have strong financial strength, rich investment experience, and a well-established internal management system. They are important additions to China's private equity market. The addition of foreign private equity funds brings in abundant capital as well as the regulated operational system of the funds. This has a demonstration effect on the development of China's private equity funds.

It is worth noting that foreign private equity fund companies have been paying more attention to the establishment of renminbi funds since 2010. BlackRock, Carlyle Group, and IDG Capital Partners have begun to raise renminbi funds. They have become an indispensable force in the renminbi private equity fund market.

Investment hotspots concentrate on the internet, clean technology, and biotechnology

New hi-technology is a popular industry of investment. Investment in the internet is keen. The seven strategic industries stated in the *12th Five-Year Plan* are favored by private equity funds. Private equity funds also invest in a wide range of industries in China. They have become an effective source of capital.

As a major financing channel in the primary market, private equity funds are a source of capital for economic entities and motivate industrial and economic development in China. This alleviates the shortage of capital in the real economy and propels the economic development and transition of China's economy.

Investments concentrate in the developed areas along the southeast coast

Developed areas along the southeast coast assume natural advantages. There is a high concentration of high-net-worth-individuals, a large regional economy, a huge pool of financial institutions and talents. A lot of promising enterprises are located in those areas and attract many private equity investment companies. This leads to a high concentration of private equity investments.

Enterprises in Jiangxi Province, Sichuan Province, Shanxi Province, and Chongqing are slowly garnering attention from private equity funds in terms of both the number and amount of investments. This helps to expand the financing channels of the regional enterprises and develop regional economies.

Launch of the growth enterprise market board and small and medium-sized enterprise board acts as a platform for the withdrawal of private equity funds through IPO

Before 2008, there were limited capital withdrawal channels in the market. Private equity funds in China withdrew from the market through mergers and acquisitions to a large extent. The return on book value was limited. The launch of the GEM and SME board offered private equity funds a channel of withdrawal through IPO. At present, IPO is the main channel of withdrawal of private equity funds. It also increases the rate of return on private equity funds 10 times.

Increasing funding difficulties, a broader private real estate investment fund market, and legal and policy risks

As a financing channel of the real estate industry, the development of private real estate investment funds is closely related to the prospects of the industry and the macroeconomic regulation and control of the industry. Under the current rigorous policies, it is difficult for real estate enterprises to secure capital on the stock and credit markets. The high cost of financing presents opportunities for private real estate investment funds to develop. However, the government has imposed stricter examination of trust type private real estate investment funds, and the funds are not yet granted legal status. From the legal and political perspective, there is a lot of uncertainty regarding the future of the funds.

9
Chapter

Recommendations on the Development of China's Privately Offered Funds

Since the first investment fund came into being in China in the early 1990s, the fund industry has been developing for 20 years. Public funds have entered into a new phase from being old funds and closed-end funds to open-end funds. Privately offered funds have experienced the stages of initial development, differentiated adjustment, the development of sunshine private funds, and are arriving at the stage of rapid development. Securities investment funds, whether public or private, are the products of the capital market. In both China and overseas, privately offered funds (private funds) are an important form of investment. Given their unique nature, their development is the natural outcome of market development.

In developed countries and regions, private funds are major institutional investors. They are an important component of the capital market. Private funds, especially hedge funds, do not only serve individual investors but are also a financial instrument for financial institutions or commercial enterprises to disperse risk or allocate assets. In China, due to factors system and the markets, the development of privately offered funds is in its early stages, and the development of hedge funds has just begun. As marketization deepens in the financial market, the development and regulation of privately offered funds have substantial meanings for and effects on China's economic development and financial reform. The development of privately offered funds, especially private equity (PE) funds, helps build the multi-layered capital market and refine the financial system. Privately offered funds mainly invest in equity rights. They can raise the proportion of direct financing in the financing structure, help small and medium-sized enterprises with financing, and optimize the economic structure. The investment strategies of privately offered funds are diversified and often include hedging strategies. This is favorable for the market to perform its functions of resource allocation and price discovery. This can raise the efficiency of the capital market. As the degree of opening up of China's economy and internationalization of the financial market increases, a lot of private funds will enter the China market. China should develop its own domestic privately offered funds to prevent foreign funds from dominating the market.

Since Reform and Opening Up, China's economy has been developing rapidly in the past 30 years. Rapid economic development brought about the increase in social wealth and household income. The professional wealth management industry emerged. In 2010, the total deposits at banks in China reached RMB72 trillion, of which RMB30.3 trillion was deposits of the residents. Many of them were high-net-worth individuals. The difference in wealth, risk tolerance, and risk preference gave rise to a diversified, personalized, and differentiated demand for financial management. Public funds and privately offered funds serve different types of clients and investors with different needs. Public funds mainly serve clients who are more conservative and have a lower risk tolerance. Privately offered funds mainly serve the more aggressive clients who have higher risk tolerance. The two types of funds complement each other.

As the financial system becomes more refined and the capital market expands, public funds and privately offered funds develop simultaneously to offer investors more investment channels. Based on our understanding of the industry and to safeguard the healthy development of the industry, recommendations on regulatory policies, industry specifications, corporate management, product innovation, and personnel training are made.

Establish an Efficient Regulation System to Provide a Favorable Policy Environment for Privately Offered Funds

In order to maintain stability, prevent and lower financial risk, protect the investors' interest, and promote the healthy growth of the industry, the information on privately offered funds should be more transparent. A well-established and efficient regulatory system suitable to the features of China's financial market should be developed. In countries whose fund industry is well developed, private funds are under regulation. Up to now, China has not developed its own philosophy and system of regulation. There are only several regulations or requirements in relevant laws.

Fairness is essential in China's regulation of privately offered funds. As major institutional investors in the capital market, privately offered funds should receive fair and just legal treatment as public funds do. Privately offered funds should be legally regulated, defined, and granted legal status. There should be a regulatory body. Regulation of privately offered funds should take into account the feature of private placement. The funds should be given flexibility. A combination of government regulation, industry and company self-regulation should be adopted. Regulation of different types of funds should be unified.

The focuses of regulation of privately offered funds should be on the entry thresholds for fund managers and investors, and information disclosure.

Entry threshold for fund managers

The entry process of privately offered fund managers should be clearly defined. Taking into account the development stages of the capital market and privately offered funds, as well as the experience of development markets, China can adopt two entry systems: the registration system and filing system.

The strictness of the entry system should depend on the size of the asset under management and number of clients of the privately offered funds. The greater the size and number, the stricter the entry threshold, and vice versa. Large privately offered funds with a considerable size of assets under management and number of clients should be required to register. Smaller funds should be filed for the record but should be allowed to register. The two systems offer fund managers some degree of choice. It should be noted that the registration system for privately offered fund managers is different from the approval system for public fund managers. The approval system is a very rigorous system. However, the registration system only needs to verify the authenticity of information. Moreover, privately offered fund managers are not required to gain approval before the launch of a product like public fund managers do. They only need to notify the relevant bodies after the launch.

Entry threshold for investors

The requirements for being a qualified investor should be clearly defined. The law of the United States gives detailed stipulation of the market entry threshold for investors and is a good example for China. Qualified investors can be classified as qualified individual investors or institutional investors. The criteria of qualified individual investors can be the annual income of the individual or family, financial assets, and investment experience. The criteria of qualified institutional investors can be the nature of the institution, total assets, net assets, and debt ratio. At present, China's privately offered funds are still in the early stages of development and the financial sense of investors is weak. The qualification conditions can be more rigorous so that only investors with great risk tolerance can qualify. This also imposes control over the scope of investors and reduces the industry risk.

The entry thresholds for fund managers and investors form a safety net in risk prevention.

Information disclosure

The degree or scope of information disclosure should vary based on the size and the market influence of the fund. Information disclosure should be mandatory for large registered privately offered funds. Information on total assets, types of assets, leverage ratio, risk evaluation, operation strategies, and valuation methods should be released. Small privately offered funds under the filing system are not required but encouraged to release information. As privately offered funds are privately placed, information is only released to the regulatory body or investors (or potential investors), but not the public. The legal liabilities regarding information disclosure should also be defined.

While the establishment of China's regulatory system of privately offered funds is underway, the trends of international finance and the features and changes of hedge funds should be analyzed. Regulatory policies more rigorous than those on domestic privately offered funds should be imposed on foreign capital entering China's privately offered fund industry. The overall financial risk should be evaluated. Regulations should be imposed on the entry threshold, scope of investment, capital flow, and withdrawal channels.

Establish a Self-Regulatory Body, Strengthen Industry Ethics and Codes of Conduct, and Promote the Healthy Development of the Industry

Privately offered funds are essentially trust funds. The industry needs to build a good reputation and gain trust from the public in order to survive and develop. Industry ethics and codes of conduct should be strengthened to guide and restrict the behavior of companies and financial practitioners for the healthy development of the industry. A professional self-regulatory body should be set up in the industry to shoulder the responsibilities. The regulatory body should also be responsible for the promotion of the industry and the education of investors in order to reinforce the investors' trust in the funds. Fund managers should abide by the rules and codes of conduct of the self-regulatory body. They should operate with the primary goal of maximizing the benefits of the investors. When there is a conflict of interest between the fund manager and investors, fund managers should not harm the interest of investors. They should preserve industry credibility. Establishing regulations and codes of conduct would curtail behavior which tarnishes the reputation of the industry, such as fraud, false promotion, false business performances, and violations of laws, regulations, and contracts. Behavior such as slander should be penalized.

Standardize Corporate Governance and Internal Control System of Privately Offered Fund Companies

After several years of development, the size of China's privately offered fund companies has increased. Despite great improvement, the governance structure of the companies is still inadequate. In order to preserve the interest of the shareholders, clients, and employees, the companies should refine and further standardize corporate governance. They should establish an organizational structure system that meets the requirements of the nature, equity structure, business features, and asset size of the companies in order to maintain sustainable development. The organizational structure should be based on the modern enterprise management methods. The duties and responsibilities of each department should be clearly defined. The quality of management should improve.

Privately offered fund companies should adopt a scientific approach toward internal control. They should optimize the investment decision-making process and a firewall system. Research, decision-making, and transactions should be independent of one another. An independent risk control department should be set up to control the risk involved in the entire investment process, before, during, and after the actual execution of an investment. A safe and stable transaction system should be set up. Professional technicians should be responsible for the maintenance of the IT system to ensure that transactions can be processed. A compliance department or internal audit department should be established to monitor the investment and business activities of the company to prevent any form of violation of laws, regulations, or contracts.

Reinforce Innovation in Product and Services to Satisfy the Diverse and Personal Financial Needs of Investors

Although there are special privately offered fund products emerging, the degree of product homogenization is high. The type, investment strategies, and investment styles of products are very similar. As investors have different asset size, income level, risk tolerance, and risk preference, they have different investment needs. Some investors are more conservative and some are more aggressive. Their target rate of return and risk tolerance differ to a large extent. Therefore, privately offered funds should research the financial needs and features of their investors before offering personalized recommendations on asset allocation. The fund managers should launch more innovative products with diversified investment strategies and investment styles in order to satisfy different types of clients.

Privately offered fund companies should provide high quality customer services and communicate with their clients. They should release operation reports and information as stated in relevant laws, regulations, and contracts. The companies should educate investors in terms of investment philosophy and the concept of financial management.

Reinforce Team Building and Improve the Professional Ethics of Practitioners

In the early stages of development of China's privately offered funds, there were little human resources because of the lack of regulation, the size of the funds, and costs. Human resources are the core resources of privately offered funds. They are the key elements of the survival and development of the funds. The companies should increase their input in team building. They should reserve human resources, formulate personnel training programs, refine the incentive mechanism, and attract talents to join the companies. The major competition in the privately offered fund industry is the competition of human resources.

Financial practitioners should improve themselves professionally. They should maintain the industry's reputation and follow the professional codes of conduct. They should be honest and diligent, put the interest of clients before their own, and abide by laws and regulations. This should help with the public image of the industry.

After several years of exploration and development, China's privately offered funds are beginning to blossom. This attracts great attention from the government and the market. This also prompts us to contemplate the future opportunities and challenges of the industry. The emergence of privately offered funds is natural and inevitable as the economy and financial market develop. China should utilize the funds as a means to increase the national wealth, improve the financial market, and develop the economy.

Notes

Chapter 5

1. Xia Bin and Chen Daofu, 2002.
2. See the *Security Act of 1933, Investment Advisers Act of 1940*, and *Investment Company Act of 1940*, http://www.sec.gov/answers/rule506.htm.
3. See the *Dodd-Frank Wall Street Reform and Consumer Protection Act*.
4. United Kingdom, Financial Services Authority, *The Collective Investment Scheme Information Guide*, http://www.fsa.gov.uk/pubs/foi/collguide.pdf.
5. United Kingdom, Financial Services Authority, *Unregulated Collective Investment Schemes*, http://www.fsa.gov.uk/smallfirms/your_firm_type/financial/pdf/ucis_factsheet.pdf; United Kingdom, *Financial Services and Markets Act 2000*, http://www.legislation.gov.uk/ukpga/2000/8/pdfs/ukpga_20000008_en.pdf.
6. United Kingdom, *Financial Services Act 2010*.
7. "Background," Hong Kong Investment Fund Association, http://www.hkifa.org.hk/eng/Background.aspx.
8. See Shou Weiguang, 2007.
9. Data from Wind Information Co., Ltd. (Wind Info).
10. International Organization of Securities Commissions, *Objectives and Principles of Securities Regulation*, http://www.iosco.org/library/pubdocs/pdf/IOSCOPD154.pdf.
11. Securities Association of China, *Zhengjuan touzi jijin* 證券投資基金 (Securities Investment Funds) (Beijing: China Financial & Economic Publishing House, 2010).
12. *Law of the People's Republic of China on Funds for Investment in Securities (Order of the President No.9)*, Chinese Government's Official Web Portal, http://english.gov.cn/laws/2005-09/07/content_29992.htm.
13. See Tebon Securities Co., Ltd. and Shanghai Security News, 2010.
14. China Banking Regulatory Commission, *Measures for the Administration of Trust Companies' Trust Plans of Aggregate Funds*, http://www.fdi.gov.cn/1800000121_39_3537_0_7.html.
15. See "Yangguang simu: Xiwang zhidao woshishei danyou simu jianguang gongmuhua" 陽光私募:希望知道我是誰 擔憂私募監管公募化 (Sunshine Private Funds: Wanting to Be Known and Concerns over Regulation), Sina Finance, http://finance.sina.com.cn/money/fund/20110131/10569335439.shtml.

Chapter 6

1. "Tractor accounts" are capital accounts which have two attached shareholder accounts.
2. This is only counting the fund products that are managed by privately offered fund companies and trust companies which were within duration. Fund products of securities companies, public funds, and banks were excluded.

3. "Fuwu jingji" 服務經濟 (Service Economy), Shanghai Statistics Website, http://www.stats-sh.gov.
    cn/frontshgl/18666/216883.html.

4. See CEIBS Lujiazui International Finance Research Center, *Zhongguo chengshi jinrong fazhan
    shuizhun pinggu fenxi kuangjia — Jiyu jinrong gongneng de shijiao* 中國城市金融發展水
    準評估分析框架—基於金融功能的視角 (Theoretical Framework for the Evaluation and
    Comparison of Chinese Cities' Financial Development), http://www.ljzfc.org/website/index.asp.

5. See TheCityUK, *Hedge Funds*.

6. Zvi Bodie, Alex Kane, and Alan J. Marcus, 2009.

7. See William F. Sharpe, 2002.

8. For the comparison of the Sortino ratio to other risk-return ratios, see Wei Jiancheng, 2010.

9. Jin Yi, 2010.

10. Ibid.

Chapter 7

1. See *Zhongguo simu zhengjuan jijin 2011 nian shangbannian baogao* 中國私募證券基金2011
    年上半年報告 (Report on China's Private Securities Funds for the First Six Months of 2011),
    Simuwang, http://www.simuwang.com/bencandy.php?fid=2&aid=68090&page=1.

2. The focus of the study was not on structured products as they rarely release information on their
    profit-sharing.

Chapter 8

1. Unless otherwise specified, PE funds refer to private equity funds in the narrow sense, VC funds
    refer to venture capital funds, and private equity funds refer to both PE and VC funds.

2. Data from the Zero2IPO Research Center analyzed by the Private Fund Research Center of Hua
    Ming Chuangfu Fund (HMC Fund).

3. See CVSource, http://english.chinaventuregroup.com.cn/database/cvsource.shtml.

4. CDH Investments appeared in the lists of top 50 VC companies and top 30 PE companies.
    Therefore, there are only 79 representative companies.

5. See the reports of the Zero2IPO Group Research Center, http://www.zero2ipogroup.com/
    research.

Bibliography

English sources

Beck, Thorsten, and Ross Levine. "Legal Institutions and Financial Development." In *Handbook for New Institutional Economics*, edited by Menard, Claude, and Mary M. Shirley. Norwell, MA: Kluwer Academic Publishers, 2005.

Credit Suisse. *2010 Hedge Fund Industry Review*. New York, 2011. https://www.credit-suisse.com/asset_management/global_includes/alternativeinvestments/doc/2010_hedge_fund_industry_review.pdf.

Diamond, Douglas W. "Monitoring and Reputation: The Choice between Bank Loans and Directly Placed Debt." *Journal of Political Economy* 99, no. 4 (1991): 689–721.

Eurekahedge. *Hedge Fund Performance Commentary — 2008 in Review*. January 2009. Accessed on July 23, 2011. http://www.eurekahedge.com/news/reports/09_jan_EHReport.pdf.

———. *The Eurekahedge Report*. January 2011. Accessed on July 23, 2011. http://www.eurekahedge.com/news/11_jan_Eurekahedge_Report_online.asp.

Gompers, Paul A. "Grandstanding in the Venture Capital Industry." *Journal of Financial Economics* 42, no. 1 (1996): 133–56.

Investment Company Institute. "Ownership of Mutual Funds, Shareholder Sentiment, and Use of the Internet, 2010." *Research Fundamentals* 19, no. 6 (2010).

———. *2011 Investment Company Fact Book*. 2011. Accessed on August 14, 2011. http://www.ici.org/pdf/2011_factbook.pdf.

La Porta, Rafael, Florecio Lopez de Silanes, Andrei Shleifer, and Robert W. Vishny. "Law and Finance." *Journal of Political Economy* 106, no. 6 (1998): 1113–15.

Mario, J. Gabelli. *The History of Hedge Funds — The Millionaire's Club*. Accessed on August 5, 2011. http://www.iamgroup.ca/doc_bin/The%20History%20of%20Hedge%20Funds%20-%20The%20Millionaires%20Club.pdf.

TheCityUK. *Hedge Funds*. May 2011. Accessed on July 25, 2011. http://www.thecityuk.com/assets/Uploads/Hedge-funds-2011.pdf.

United States Securities and Exchange Commission. *Implications of the Growth of Hedge Funds.* September 29, 2003. Accessed on August 16, 2011. http://www.sec.gov/news/studies/hedgefunds0903.pdf.

Wilson, John W. *The New Ventures: Inside the High-Stakes World of Venture Capital.* Addison-Wesley, 1986.

Translated sources

Bodie, Zvi, Alex Kane, and Alan J. Marcus. *Touzixue* 投資學 (Investments). Beijing: China Machine Press, 2009.

Chen Ning 陳寧. "Youxian hehuo falü zhidu yanjiu" 有限合夥法律制度研究 (Study on the Legal System of Limited Partnership). Master's thesis, Dongbei University of Finance and Economics, 2006.

Chen Peng 陳鵬. "Zhengjuan touzi jijin jingliren tezheng yu jijin jixiao guanxi yanjiu" 證券投資基金經理人特徵與基金績效關係研究 (Study on the Relationship between the Features of Securities Investment Fund Managers and the Performance of the Funds). Master's thesis, University of International Business and Economics, 2007.

Chen Qiwei 陳奇偉, and Xu Yangyang 胥楊洋. "Woguo simujijin fengxian kongzhi de falü duice" 我國私募基金風險控制的法律對策 (China's Legal Measures Pertaining to Risk Control of Privately Offered Funds). *Nanchang daxue xuebao (renwen shehuikexue ban)* 南昌大學學報(人文社會科學版) (Journal of Nanchang University (Humanities and Social Sciences)) 1 (2010).

Chen Yehong 陳業宏, and Huang Yuanyuan 黃媛媛. "Gongsizhi yu youxian hehuozhi fengxian touzi zhi bijiao yu xuanze" 公司制與有限合夥制風險投資之比較與選擇 (Comparison and Choice between the Corporate System and Limited Partnership of Venture Capital Funds). *Huazhong shifan daxue (renwen shehuikexue ban)* 華中師範大學 (人文社會科學版) (Journal of Central China Normal University (Humanities and Social Sciences)) 42, no. 6 (2003)

China Economic Herald, and WEFore Investment Consulting Company. *2008 nian fangdichan jinrong hangye fengxian fenxi baogao* 2008年房地產金融行業風險分析報告 (Risk Analysis of Real Estate Financial Industry 2008).

———. *2010 nian fangdichan jinrong hangye fengxian fenxi baogao* 2010年房地產金融行業風險分析報告 (Risk Analysis of Real Estate Financial Industry 2010).

China Securities Regulatory Commission. *Zhongguo ziben shichang fazhan baogao* 中國資本市場發展報告 (China Capital Markets Development Report). Beijing: China Financial Publishing House, 2008.

Chou Xiaohui 仇曉慧. *Simu jianghu* 私募江湖 (The Privately Offered Funds). Beijing: CITIC Publishing House, 2010.

Engerman, Stanley L., and Robert E. Gallman, eds. *Jianqiao Meiguo jinjishi (Disanjuan): 20 shiji* 劍橋美國經濟史（第三卷）：20世紀 (Cambridge Economic History of the United States, Volume III: The Twentieth Century). Beijing: China Renmin University Press, 2008.

Gao Hongye 高鴻業. *Xifang jingjixue* 西方經濟學 (Western Economics). Beijing: China Renmin University Press, 2011.

Guo Mingshan 郭明衫, Yang Bo 楊波, and Sun Changxiong 孫長雄. "Fengxian touzi youxian hehuozhi jili yuesu jizhi yanjiu" 風險投資有限合夥制激勵約束機制研究 (The Incentive Mechanism and Constraint Mechanism of Venture Capital Limited Partnership). *Shanye yanjiu* 商業研究 (Commercial Research) 2 (2008).

Hong Kong Exchanges and Clearing Limited. *Cash Market Transaction Survey 2009/10*. February 2011. Accessed on June 21, 2011. http://www.hkex.com.hk/eng/stat/research/Documents/cmts10.pdf.

Hong Yuan 洪淵. "Kaifang tiaojian xia simujijin de gongneng yu fengxian kongzhi" 開放條件下私募基金的功能與風險控制 (The Function and Risk Control of the Private Fund in an Open Economy). *Caijing kexue* 財經科學 (Finance & Economics) 2 (2007).

Jin Yi 金一. "Yangguang simujijin guonei shichang yingxiao moshi yanjiu" 陽光私募基金國內市場行銷模式研究 (Research on the Marketing Model for Sunshine Private Offering Fund in the China Market). Master's thesis, Lanzhou University, 2010.

Li Anfang 李安方. "Meiguo simujijin de yunzuo jizhi" 美國私募基金的運作機制 (Operation Mechanism of the U.S. Private Funds). *Zhengjuan shichang daobao* 證券市場導報 (Securities Market Herald) 5 (2001).

Li Simin 李思敏. "Woguo simujijin zhidu chuangxin ji jianguan wenti yanjiu" 我國私募基金制度創新及監管問題研究 (Innovations and Regulatory Problems of China's Privately Offered Fund System). *Jinrong yu jingji* 金融與經濟 (Finance and Economy) 6 (2007).

Liang Ruihan 梁銳漢. "Mogendatong qishilu: Yinhangxi jijin gongsi tuwei zhi dao" 摩根大通啟示錄: 銀行系基金公司突圍之道 (Revelations of JP Morgan Chase: How Fund Companies of Banks Breakout). Accessed on June 25, 2011. http://cn.morningstar.com/article/AR00003696.

Ling Huawei 淩華薇, and Yu Ning 于甯. "Xu Weiguo bingbai hefang" 徐衛國兵敗何方 (Why Xu Weiguo Failed). *Caijing* 財經 (Caijing Magazine), January 24, 2005.

Liu Xiaocun 劉曉純, and Shen Hao 沈浩. "Lun youxian hehuo zai woguo fengxian touzi lingyu de zhidu jiazhi" 論有限合夥在我國風險投資領域的制度價值 (The Value of Limited Partnership in Venture Capital). *Zhongyang caijing daxue xuebao* 中央財經大學學報 (Journal of Central University of Finance & Economics) 11 (2009).

Liu Zhiyang 劉志陽, and Shi Zuliu 施祖留. "Fengxian touzi jijin zhili jiegou de zhidu bianqian" 風險投資基金治理結構的制度變遷 (Institutional Change of Governance Structure of Venture Fund). *Zhengjuan shichang daobao* 證券市場導報 (Securities Market Herald) 7 (2005).

Lu Xianxiang 盧現祥. *Xifang zhidu jingjixue* 西方新制度經濟學 (Western Institutional Economics). Beijing: China Development Press, 2003.

Luo Yongxin 雒永信. "Guanli fudu de lilun tantao" 管理幅度的理論探討 (Theoretical Discussion of the Scope of Management). *Shanghai qiye* 上海企業 (Shanghai Business) 8 (2006).

Ma Qingquan 馬慶泉, and Wu Qing 吳清, eds. *Zhongguo zhengjuan shi (diyi juan) (1978–1998 nian)* 中國證券史(第一卷)（1978－1998年） (China Securities History I, 1978–1998). Beijing: China Financial Publishing House, 2009.

——, eds. *Zhongguo zhengjuan shi (dier juan) (1999–2007 nian)* 中國證券史(第二卷)（1999－2007年） (China Securities History II, 1999–2007). Beijing: China Financial Publishing House, 2009.

North, Douglas C. *Zhidu, zhidu bianqian yu jingji jixiao* 制度、制度變遷與經濟績效 (Institutions, Institutional Change and Economic Performance). Shanghai: Shanghai Joint Publishing Company and Shanghai People's Publishing House, 2008.

Pei Linlin 裴琳琳. "Zhongguo simujijin fengxian kongzhi yanjiu" 中國私募基金風險控制研究 (Study on the Risk Control of China Venture Capital Funds). Master's thesis, China University of Political Science and Law, 2008.

Peng Ya 彭雅. "Lun woguo simujijin falü zhidu de goujian" 論我國私募基金法律制度的構建 (Construction of China's Legal System Pertaining to Privately Offered Funds). Master's thesis, Hunan University, 2007.

Peng Yiping 彭怡萍, Yang Tao 楊濤, and Ge Xinyuan 葛新元. "Yangguang simujijin yunying moshi chuangxin tanxi" 陽光私募基金運營模式創新探析 (Investigation of the Innovations of the Operating Model of Sunshine Private Funds). *Ziben shichang* 資本市場 (Capital Markets) 4 (2010).

Research and Statistics Department, Economic and Industrial Policy Bureau, Ministry of Economy, Trade and Industry. *Guoneiwai riyi zengduo de duichong jijin shiji zhuangkuang diaocha baogao* 國內外日益增多的對沖基金實際狀況調查報告 (Research Report on the Increasing Number of Domestic and Foreign Hedge Funds). Accessed on July 23, 2011.

"Rongzhi pingji — Zhongguo simu zhengjuan jijin 2011 shangbannian baogao" 融智評級 — 中國私募證券基金2011上半年報告 (The Rongzhi Rating System: Half Yearly Report on China's Private Securities Investment Funds 2011). Simuwang. Accessed on July 18, 2011. http://www.simuwang.com/bencandy.php?fid=2&id=68090.

Securities and Futures Commission. *Zhengjianhui chipai jijin jingli/guwen de duichong jijin huodong diaocha baogao* 證監會持牌基金經理/顧問的對沖基金活動調查報告 (Report on the Survey on Hedge Fund Activities of SFC-licensed Managers/Advisers). March 2011. Accessed on June 21, 2011. http://www.sfc.hk/web/doc/TC/speeches/public/surveys/11/Hedge%20fund%20managers_201103c.pdf.

———. *2010 nian huanqiu ji Xianggang zhengjuan shichang huigu* 2010年環球及香港證券市場回顧 (A Review of the Global and Local Securities Markets in 2010). January 27, 2011. Accessed on June 21, 2011. http://www.sfc.hk/web/doc/TC/research/research/RS%20Paper%2048%20(chi).pdf.

———. *2010 nian jijin guanli huodong diaocha* 2010年基金管理活動調查 (Fund Management Activities Survey 2010). July 2011. http://www.sfc.hk/web/doc/TC/speeches/public/surveys/11/fmas_201107_chi.pdf.

Securities Association of China. *2009 Zhongguo zhengjuan touzi jijinye nianbao* 2009中國證券投資基金業年報 (2009 China Securities Investment Funds Fact Book). Beijing: Economic Science Press, 2010.

Sharpe, William F. *Touzixue* 投資學 (Investments). Beijing: China Renmin University Press, 2002.

Shi Haixia 史海霞. "Guanyu guanli fudu yu guanli cengci de zuzhi jiegou moxing yanjiu" 關於管理幅度與管理層次的組織結構模型研究 (Research on Organizational Structure Model Concerned with Administrative Extent and Level). *Xi'nan keji daxue xuebao (zhexue shehuikexue ban)* 西南科技大學學報（哲學社會科學版）(Journal of Southwest University of Science and Technology (Philosophy and Social Science Edition) 4 (2008).

Shou Weiguang 壽偉光. *Lun jijin jianguan zhengce* 論基金監管政策 (Regulatory Policies of Funds). Shanghai: Fudan University Press, 2007.

Sun Zhanghua 孫長華. "Woguo hehuazhi simujijin fazhan wenti yanjiu" 我國合夥制私募基金發展問題研究 (Study on the Developmental Issues of China's Privately Offered Funds under the Partnership System). *Xiandai guanli kexue* 現代管理科學 (Modern Management Science) 4 (2011).

Sun Xiaojie 孫曉潔. "Zhongguo hehuozhi simujijin de fazhan zhanlüe sikao" 中國合夥制私募基金的發展戰略思考 (Developmental Strategies of China's Privately Offered Funds under the Partnership System). *Zhongguo shichang* 中國市場 (China Market) 13 (2011).

Tebon Securities Co., Ltd., and Shanghai Security News. *Zhongguo 2010 yangguang simu niandu baogao* 中國2010陽光私募年度報告 (Report on China's Sunshine Private Funds 2010). Nanjing: Jiangsu Renmin Press, 2010

The Investment Trusts Association, Japan. *Riben touzi xintuo 2011* 日本投資信託2011 (Japan's Investment Trusts 2011). Accessed on July 23, 2011. http://www.toushin.or.jp/index.php.

Wang Kaixia 王凱霞, and Xing Yu 刑昱. "Duichong jijinye de xinfazhan ji qi jianguan tansuo" 對沖基金業的新發展及其監管探索 (New Development of and Regulation on Hedge Funds). *Huabei jinrong* 華北金融 (Huabei Finance) 6 (2010).

Wang Taiqiang 王泰強, and Hou Guangming 侯光明. "Simujijin yangguanghua zhi lu" 私募基金的陽光化之路 (The Legalization Process of Private-Funds). *Beijing ligong daxue xuebao (Shehuikexue ban)* 北京理工大學學報（社會科學版）(Journal of Beijing Institute of Technology (Social Sciences Edition)) 4 (2009).

Wei Jiancheng 魏建成. "Kaifangshi gupiaojijin yeji pingjia — Jiyu Sortino bilü yu chuantong yeji pingjia zhibiao de fenxi" 開放式股票基金業績評價 — 基於Sortino比率與傳統業績評價指標的分析 (Evaluation of the Performance of Open-End Stock Funds: Analysis Based on the Sortino Ratio and Traditional Performance Evaluation Indexes). *Xiandai shangye* 現代商業 (Modern Business) 6 (2010).

Wu Kai 武凱. "Jijin guanlifei zhidu anpai de jili xiaoying yu youhua xuanze" 基金管理費制度安排的激勵效應與優化選擇 (Incentives on Funds Management Fee and Optimized Option). *Zhengjuan shichang daobao* 證券市場導報 (Securities Market Herald) 8 (2005).

Xia Bin 夏斌, and Chen Daofu 陳道富. *Zhongguo simujijin baogao* 中國私募基金報告 (Report on Private Equity Funds in China). Shanghai: Shanghai Far East Press, 2002.

Xiao Xinrong 肖欣榮. "Zhongguo zhengjuan touzi jijin guanliren xingwei yanjiu" 中國證券投資基金管理人行為研究 (Probing into the Manager's Behavior of China's Securities Investment Fund). *Jinrong lilun yu shijian* 金融理論與實踐 (Financial Theory and Practice) 3 (2004).

Xie Tianjiao 解天驕. "Guonei yangguang simujijin xianzhuang yu fazhan quishi tanxi" 國內陽光私募基金現狀與發展趨勢探析 (The Present and Future Development of Sunshine Private Funds in China). *Quanguo shangqing (Jingji lilun yanjiu)* 全國商情 (經濟理論研究) (China Business) 11 (2010).

Xue Hesheng 薛和生, Zheng Bo 鄭波, and Fu Qiang 傅強. "Lun woguo simujijin yangguanghua" 論我國私募基金陽光化 (The Trend of Privately Raised Fund in China Becoming More Transparent). *Shanghai shifan daxue xuebao (Zhexue shehuikexue ban)* 上海師範大學學報 (哲學社會科學版) (Journal of Shanghai Normal University (Philosophy & Social Sciences Edition)) 4 (2008).

Yang Gongpu 楊公朴, and Xia Dawei 夏大慰. *Chanye jingjixue jiaocheng* 產業經濟學教程 (Guide to Industrial Economics). Shanghai: Shanghai University of Finance and Economics Press, 2008.

Yang Guangning 楊廣宇. "Jijin hunhe guanlifei jili zhidu sheji ji qi shizheng fenxi" 基金混合管理費激勵制度設計及其實證分析 (Empirical Analysis of the Design of the Incentive Mechanism of Funds Based on Administration Fee). Master's thesis, Jinan University, 2008.

Ye Chuancai 葉傳財, and Pan Lianxiang 潘連鄉. "Fengxian touzi jijin jingliren tezhi yu jijin touzi jixiao guanlianxing yanjiu" 風險投資基金經理人特質與基金投資績效關聯性研究 (The Relationship between the Features of Venture Capital Fund Managers and the Fund's Performance). *Shangye shidai* 商業時代 (Commercial Times) 13 (2011).

Ye Xiang 葉翔. "Zhongguo simu zhengjuan touzi jijin de xianzhuang yu fazhan yanjiu" 中國私募證券投資基金的現狀與發展研究 (Study on the Present and Future Development of Private Securities Investment Funds in China). Master's thesis, Xiamen University, 2002.

Yin Jie 殷潔. "Simujijin de hefahua ji qi fengxian kongzhi" 私募基金的合法化及其風險控制 (Legalization and Risk Control of Privately Offered Funds). *Jinrong yu jingji* 金融與經濟 (Finance and Economy) 11 (2004).

Yu Hongkai 于宏凱. "Jijin jingliren jili jizhi jiexi" 基金經理人激勵機制解析 (Analysis of the Incentive Mechanism of Fund Managers). *Zhengjuan shichang daobao* 證券市場導報 (Securities Market Herald) 1 (2003).

Yu Ning 于甯, Wu Xiaoliang 吳小亮, and Ling Huawei 凌華薇, "Dapeng zhi mo" 大鵬之歿 (The Demise of Dapeng). *Caijing* 財經 (Caijing Magazine), January 24, 2005.

Yu Ping 于萍. "Bianpinghua zuzhi xiaolü fenxi" 扁平化組織效率分析 (Analysis of the Organizational Efficiency of a Flattened Structure). *Zhongguo shichang* 中國市場 (China Market) 18 (2007).

Zero2IPO Research Center. *Zhongguo chuangtou ji simu guquan touzi shichang 2010 shuju huigu* 中國創投暨私募股權投資市場2010資料回顧 (Data Review of the China Venture Capital and private Equity Markets 2010).

———. *2011 nian dier jidu Zhongguo chuangye touzi yanjiu baogao* 2011年第二季度中國創業投資研究報告 (China Venture Capital Report 02 2011). Accessed on August 23, 2011. http://research.pedaily.cn/report/pay/613.shtml.

———. *2011 nian dier jidu Zhongguo simu guquan touzi yanjiu baogao* 2011年第二季度中國私募股權投資研究報告 (China Private Equity Report 02 2011). Accessed on August 23, 2011. http://research.pedaily.cn/report/pay/614.shtml.

Zhang Wei 張煒, and Meng Haojie 孟昊桀. "Chaoyue juxian, mianlin guaidian — Yangguang simujijin chanpin fenxi" 超越局限，面臨拐點 — 陽光私募基金產品分析 (At a Turning Point and Beyond: Analysis of Sunshine Private Fund Products). *Guoji jinrong* 國際金融 (International Finance) 3 (2011).

Zhao Di 趙迪. *Ziben de jueqi: Zhongguo gushi ershinian de fengyu lu* 資本的崛起：中國股市二十年風雲錄 (The Rise of the Capital Market: The Past 20 Years of the China Stock Market). Beijing: China Machine Press, 2011.

Zhao Jinlu 趙瑾璐, and Cui Shunquan 崔順全. "Youxian hehuozhi de zuzhi youshi fenxi" 有限合夥制的組織優勢分析 (The Advantages of Limited Partnership). *Beijing ligong daxue xuebao (shehuikexue ban)* 北京理工大學學報（社會科學版）(Journal of Beijing Institute of Technology (Social Sciences Edition)) 8 (2005).

Zhu Qifeng 朱奇峰. *Zhongguo simu guquan jijin lilun、shijian yu qianjian* 中國私募股權基金理論、實踐與前瞻 (Theory, Practices and Prospect of China's Private Equity Fund Development). Beijing: Tsinghua University Press, 2010.

Index

A-share market 39, 54, 56

absolute return 72

accounts 13, 21, 26, 28, 31, 34, 38, 73, 91, 161-2

accredited investors 4, 16-19

acquisitions 92-4, 143, 146-7, 157

administration fee 49, 94, 117-23, 125

agents 86, 107

annual income 15, 33, 162

annual rate of return 56, 64

annualized rate of return 63-4, 118

approval 23-4, 26, 30, 34, 100, 162

Asia 9-10

asset allocation 59, 104-5, 165

asset size 39, 52, 113, 162, 164

assets 5, 16, 19, 23, 32-4, 38, 40, 52, 67, 93, 107, 160, 162-3

assets under management (AUM) 5, 23, 38, 52, 162

average rate of return 55-8, 64, 70, 117, 154

Bank of China 23-4, 29

banks 12, 15, 20, 39, 59, 82, 86-8, 90, 110, 160

Beijing 45-8, 53, 129-30, 141-2, 149-50

bond funds 51, 122

brokerage collection management 56, 86

brokerages 57, 59-61, 87, 107, 109

bull market 55, 64, 76

business performance 43, 83, 86, 92, 94, 109

capital 4, 6-7, 18, 20, 23, 27, 31, 48-9, 82, 148, 154-7

capital asset pricing model (CAPM) 77

capital market 2-3, 9, 12, 23, 26, 30, 48, 59, 88, 102, 107, 160-2

central figures 105-12

China 2, 4, 6, 20-6, 28-32, 34-5, 37-94, 102, 106, 122-6, 136, 142-4, 148-52, 154-7, 159-65

China Banking Regulatory Commission (CBRC) 29, 31-4, 152

China market 20, 40, 154, 160

classification 53, 148-9

clients 5, 26, 32, 59, 87-8, 161-2, 164-5

codes of conduct 163

collective investment schemes 6-8, 10, 19-20

collective trust funds 32, 50, 91

companies 4, 16, 42-4, 52, 83, 85-6, 90, 94, 96-9, 101-2, 104-7, 111-17, 127-8, 148-51, 163-5

comparison 13-19, 21, 47-8, 55, 61-3, 66-7, 77-8, 97-9, 121-2, 126-7, 137

competition 53, 86-7, 94, 128, 156, 165

contracts 12, 19, 29, 102, 122, 124, 163-5

costs 90-1, 93-4, 106, 128, 154, 165

credit risk 102

CSRC (China Securities Regulatory Commission) 21, 24-5, 28-31, 34

custodian 25, 29, 82, 90, 121

custodian banks 25, 28-30, 32, 89

custodian fee 118, 120-2

decision-making committee 100, 112

decision-making process 22, 96, 100-1, 164

development 2, 9-11, 47-8, 50-1, 82-3, 97-9, 101-2, 106-7, 114-17, 128, 136, 148-9, 154-5, 160, 164-5

Dodd-Frank Wall Street Reform and Consumer Protection Act 3, 5, 13, 17, 19

downside risk 54, 66, 72-7, 79-80, 105-6

duration 23, 50, 92, 121

economic activities 46, 52
economic development 156, 160
economic growth 14
economic transition 20-1
economic zone 43-4
economy 11, 13-14, 121, 165
education 29, 107, 116, 140, 144-5, 163
employees 41-2, 94, 97, 103, 106-7, 115-16, 150, 164
enterprises 52, 99, 156
entry systems 162
entry threshold 15, 17, 22, 34, 161-3
equity rights 151, 153, 160
equity transfer 143, 146
European Union (EU) 6-7, 13
evaluation 13, 47-8, 73, 77, 104, 155
exemption 5, 7-8, 13, 17
experience 4, 12, 15, 24, 33, 35, 42, 87-8, 92, 109, 111-12, 116, 150, 162

female members 113-15
financial crisis 136, 138
financial development 46-7
financial industry 2, 6, 14, 32, 47
Financial Industry Regulatory Authority (FINRA) 3
financial institutions 4, 14-15, 20-1, 23, 28, 45-8, 87, 97-8, 110, 156, 160
financial liberalization 6
financial market 2, 14, 20, 35, 45-6, 82-3, 160-1, 165
financial practitioners 31, 40, 42-3, 48, 107, 109, 163, 165
financial products 21, 47, 49, 88
financial reform 2, 4, 160
financial regulation 2
Financial Services and Markets Act 6-8, 17-19
Financial Services Authority (FSA) 7-8, 14, 19-20
Financial Stability Oversight Council (FSOC) 3-5, 19
financial system 8, 20, 22, 160-1

financing channels 85, 136, 152, 154, 156-7
first echelon 52, 67-8, 70, 73-4, 76
fixed ratio 122-3, 125-7
floating rates 126-7
floating ratio 123-7
fluctuation 14, 27, 54, 56, 64, 66-72, 83, 121
Forbes 45
foreign capital 148-9, 154, 163
foreign companies 148-9
foreign currencies 137, 139
foreign investments 89, 136
former public fund managers 59-61, 83, 87, 107, 109, 128
functional departments 96, 98
fund companies 38-9, 41-6, 48-50, 52-3, 82-3, 85-8, 91-4, 96-7, 99, 102, 106-7, 114-17, 123, 128, 164-5
fund industry 2-3, 6, 9, 13, 20-1, 25-30, 32, 35, 37, 41-3, 51-3, 77, 81-3, 91, 160-1
fund management companies 25-6, 30, 38, 50, 58, 89, 121, 154
fund managers 11, 29, 31, 42-3, 59, 85-7, 92, 94, 100, 102-5, 107-8, 110-12, 115-16, 123-7, 161-3
fundraising 121, 136-7
futures markets 9-10

general manager 97, 104, 106
government 6-9, 23, 32, 48, 102, 136, 149, 155, 157, 165
grassroots 60-1, 107, 109
growth 2, 38-9, 62, 85, 92, 94, 115-17, 138, 143, 155
growth enterprise market (GEM) 143, 146-7
growth rates 39, 46, 91, 137-8
guarantees 33, 47, 49, 87, 96, 103

headquarters 24, 47, 149
hedge funds 2-3, 5, 8-11, 14, 40, 49, 51, 87, 91, 160, 163

Herfindahl-Hirschman Index (HHI) 52-3
hierarchy 98
high-net-worth individuals, (HNWIs) 8, 14, 34, 45-6, 87, 160
Hong Kong 9-11, 13-17, 20, 47, 149-50
Hong Kong Investment Funds Association (HKIFA) 9
human resources 42, 47, 106, 115-17, 128, 148, 150, 165
hybrid funds 51

incentive mechanisms 43, 48, 108, 116, 151, 165
income 16, 123-6
individual investors 17, 160
information disclosure 3, 5, 8, 10-11, 13, 15, 19-20, 22, 25, 29-30, 32-4, 82, 91, 102, 161-3
initial development 30, 160
institutional investors 26, 160-2
insurance companies 12, 15, 59, 87, 107, 110
interests 22, 26-7, 31, 102, 161, 163-5
intermediaries 15, 86
Internal risk control 22, 103-6, 128
international financial centers 47-8
internet 140-1, 143-5, 156
intestacy 8, 15
Investment Advisers Act 2-5, 10
investment behaviors 91, 100
investment capabilities 39, 58
investment channels 155, 161
investment companies 2, 8, 136
Investment Company Act 2-4, 10
Investment Company Institute (ICI) 3
investment consultants 31-2, 34, 49, 82, 89, 122
investment funds 2-3, 6, 8-9, 11, 13-14, 22-4, 26-7, 136
investment philosophy 30-1, 81, 94, 165
investment professionals 8, 150
investment research 98, 107, 113, 128
investment research teams 42, 99, 105-7, 112-16

investment scope 83, 163
investment stages 151
investment strategies 33, 45, 59, 85, 160, 164
investment threshold 85, 153
investment trusts 11-12, 14, 18, 24
investment vehicles 4, 34
investments 11-12, 15, 18, 30-1, 50-1, 87-91, 100-1, 103-4, 106-7, 112, 136, 138-42, 151-3, 156, 163-4
investors 3, 8-9, 11-12, 15-19, 22, 26-7, 29-32, 49-50, 82-3, 85-7, 89-90, 99, 102-3, 120-9, 161-5
IPO 88, 143, 146-7, 157
IPO withdrawals 146

Japan 11-20
joint stock companies 6

Law on Securities Investment Fund 26, 30-2
laws 2, 4, 6, 10-11, 13, 15-17, 21-2, 26, 28-35, 50, 82, 102, 111, 162-5
legal regulations 2, 13, 26-7, 32, 50
legal rights 28-9
legal status 26, 31, 34, 82, 102, 128, 151
legislation 3, 8-10, 13-14, 22, 27, 34
leverage 4, 12, 19, 102-3
limited partners 50, 89
limited partnership 49-50, 85, 89-90, 148, 150-1, 154-5
limited partnership companies 33, 49, 85, 89, 91, 148
liquidation 92-4
liquidity risk 102-3, 105
local governments 23-4
lock-up period 118-19, 121, 153
loss 48, 55-6, 61, 73, 92, 94, 102, 123-4, 126

macroeconomic regulation 8, 152, 157
management 5, 22, 24, 33, 52, 96, 98-9, 103, 111-13, 132, 162, 164

management range 98-9
management structure 96
market competition 52, 81
market concentration 52
market development 30, 136, 160
market feedback 100
market manipulation 26-7, 31
market operations 109
market participants 13, 27, 52
market recognition 32, 38, 83
market regulation 9
market shock 55, 61, 76
mature markets 2, 13, 20, 35
maturity 92-3, 124, 151
mergers 92-4, 143, 146-7, 157
minimum guarantee 123-7
money market funds 51, 122

National Association of Securities Dealers
    (NASD) 3
National People's Congress 26, 31-2
natural person 16, 33
net assets 15-16, 40, 43, 162
non-accredited investors 4

operation 15, 18, 22, 24-31, 34, 42-3, 50,
    82, 89, 92, 96-7, 102, 113
operational risk 100, 102-3, 105
organizational structure 96-9, 164
overseas markets 6, 56, 129

partners 49, 90
PE funds 136-9, 146-8
People's Bank of China 23-4, 29
performance 38, 43, 49, 54, 56-7, 60-2, 64,
    77, 87, 94, 100, 107, 120, 122-3
personnel training 106, 115, 128, 161
portfolio 31, 78-9
positions 55, 73, 101, 103-5, 116
preferential tax policies 48-9
pressure 83, 86, 93
private banks 88, 94
private capital 148-9

private equity (PE) 22, 42, 136-7, 139, 143,
    147, 152, 154-5, 160
private equity investment companies
    148-51, 156
private fund industry 34, 52-3, 92-3, 115
private fund managers 4, 10, 17, 59-61
private fund markets 3, 14, 50
private fund products 46, 49-51, 53, 68-
    70, 73-6, 78-9, 81, 85, 87-8, 91-3, 105,
    117-18, 121-2, 124, 126
private funds 2-7, 9-15, 17-23, 31-5, 38-
    40, 42-3, 49-52, 54-61, 63-7, 70-4, 76-8,
    80-4, 86-94, 127-9, 160-1
private investment trusts 11-12, 17-19
private placements 17, 85, 161
private real estate investment funds 136,
    152-3, 157
private securities investment fund
    companies 82, 95-7, 99, 101-3, 105-7,
    109, 111, 113, 115, 117, 119, 121, 123,
    125, 127-9
private securities investment funds 32, 34,
    38, 48, 54, 81, 83, 102-3, 106, 127, 129,
    136
professional investors 12, 16
profits 6, 33, 107, 117, 119, 122-6, 151
public fund companies 41-2, 94, 97, 99,
    101, 110-15, 121-2
public fund managers 43, 55, 107, 162
public hedge funds 10-11, 14

qualified individual investors 162
qualified institutional investors 12, 15-16,
    18, 162

rate of return 54-5, 57-8, 60-2, 64-6, 70,
    72-3, 76, 78-80, 116, 123-6, 147, 157
real estate 88, 140-1, 145, 152, 154
redemption 50, 117-21
redemption fee 117-22
reform 5-6, 20, 160
regional GDP 46
registration 3-5, 7, 17, 19, 43, 49

registration system 162
regulations 4-7, 9-13, 15, 20, 22, 24-8, 30, 32, 34-5, 82, 91, 96, 152, 161, 163-5
regulatory bodies 21-2, 24, 27-9, 34, 38, 161, 163
regulatory policies 27, 161, 163
regulatory system 2-6, 9, 11, 13, 15, 20-6, 34, 82, 107, 163
Renminbi 137-9, 156
repurchases 143, 146-7
research 58, 100-1, 104, 109, 116, 152, 164
researchers 40, 42-3, 60, 94, 101, 112, 115-16, 150
risk 4, 20, 28, 49-50, 66-7, 70, 72-4, 77-8, 80, 88, 102-6, 113, 164
risk management 4, 91, 100-2
risk-return distribution 68-70
risk tolerance 160, 164

sales channels 86, 88, 98, 109, 128
secondary market 32, 85, 103
securities 2, 4, 9-10, 12, 15-18, 27, 31, 50, 90, 94, 101
Securities and Exchange Commission 3, 17-19
Securities and Futures Commission (SFC) 9-11, 14
Securities and Futures Ordinance 9-10, 17-19
Securities Association of China (SAC) 25, 28-9, 41-2
securities companies 3, 39, 97
securities markets 23-4, 30, 32, 102-3, 109
segregated account management products 34, 85
self-regulation 3, 5, 7, 21, 27-8
self-regulatory bodies 3, 9, 21, 28, 163
Shanghai 23, 43, 45-8, 133, 141-2, 149-50
sharing ratio 117-20, 122, 124-7
Sharpe ratio 77-80
Shenzhen 44, 46-8, 142, 149-50
sophisticated investors 8, 15
Sortino ratio 77, 79-81

SSE Composite Index 54-5
State Council Securities Commission (SCSC) 24
stock exchange 3, 7, 9, 15, 23, 28-9, 47, 83, 146
stock funds 51, 122
stock pool 100-1, 103, 105
stocks 28, 32, 83, 87, 110, 157
strategies 21, 72, 94, 100, 106
structured products 49-50, 61-2, 93, 96, 127
sunshine private funds 22, 31-2, 34, 38-40, 42-3, 45-6, 49-52, 54-61, 63-89, 91-4, 96-103, 105, 110-18, 121-2, 125-34
SZITIC Pure Heart China Investment Trust 31, 38, 82

third-party financial institutions 86-8
total assets 2, 15, 19, 23, 52, 162-3
total investment 138-9
traders 59, 90, 100, 103, 105
transactions 4, 8, 29, 32-3, 89, 164
Treynor ratio 77
trust companies 32-4, 38, 51, 59, 89-91, 94, 97, 107, 110, 116, 152
trust funds 30, 91, 119, 152, 163
trust of trust 50, 89, 91
trustees 8, 15, 24, 32-3, 89-90, 122
trusts 8, 11-12, 15-16, 32, 50, 82, 85, 88, 91, 116, 153, 163

underground funds 32
unstructured products 49-50, 61-2, 91, 93, 125-7

value-added services 140-1, 143-5
venture capital funds 5, 19, 48

Wall Street Crash 2
withdrawals 14, 103, 136, 143-5, 147, 157

year-on-year growth 136

CPSIA information can be obtained at www.ICGtesting.com
Printed in the USA
BVOW07*0800040614

355321BV00003B/21/P

9 781623 200077